Contents

Section 4: Planning and Executing Your Dive

Section 5: Your Underwater World

Section 6: Your Scuba Diving Experiences and Beyond

Appendix

Acknowledgements

Editor in Chief	Robert A. Clark
Manager of Development	James E. Bruning
Consultants	Ed Christini, Gary Clark, Pat Dunn Doug McNeese, Kirk Mortensen, Eric Peterson, Dennis Pulley, Ed Salamone
Graphic Designers	Lori Evans, OWD Art Director Kimberly Watts, OWD Senior Designer Jennifer Shurtleff
Cover Photos	Keith Ibsen, Bernd Rac
Photographers	Robert Aukerman, James E. Bruning, Lori Evans, Blake Miller, Randy Pfizenmaier, Bernd Rac
Contributing Editors	James E. Bruning, Gary Clark, Jean Gallagher, Doug McNeese, Steve Newman, Jeff Powelson
Technical Editors	Walt Amidon, Rusty Berry, Larry Cox Martin Denison, Watson DeVore, Dave Farrar, Jean Gallagher, Joe Gaydeski, Jere Hallenbeck, Mike Holbrook, Bob Holston, Bruce Hootman, Bill Hooven, Dohn Hubley, Harrison Jenkins, Michael McCrory, Steve Newman, Andy Ogburn, Larry Ogburn, Frank Palmero, Don Peterson, Jeff Powelson, Mike Van Hosen, Paul Wagenseller, Craig Willemsen, Randy Wright

Special thanks to Jean Gallagher, Lori Evans and Doug McNeese, without whom the vision of this manual would have not come to fruition.

Preface

You will see that each section includes several unique icons to highlight information or add information that relates to the text near it. In some cases, these icons point out information directly associated with the section objectives, while in other cases, the icon indicates a continuing education opportunity. While these icons are designed to help you learn and retain information, they also provide you with an easy reference to important information as you study.

Pearl

"Pearl" the oyster (originally named "Hey!"), is found throughout the text to point out information that we believe is key to a new diver's success. The "pearls of wisdom" that our oyster friend highlights are designed to help you meet section objectives, assist in answering study guide questions and may be used in group discussions with your instructor.

Continuing Education

At Scuba Schools International, we believe that one of the keys to achieving and maintaining success as a diver is taking the "next step" via continuing education. To reinforce that belief, we have put a Continuing Education icon next to topics that correspond to continuing education opportunities available to you through your SSI Dealer. Your SSI Instructor or Dealer will be happy to answer any questions you may have about the continuing education courses listed throughout this manual.

Environment

SSI has always supported and promoted environmental awareness and believes that care for the environment should be a standard part of diver education from start to finish. For these reasons, an environmental icon has been included to highlight important environmental issues as they relate to divers and the underwater world. Topics that you will find the environmental icon next to include the importance of buoyancy control, reef appreciation and conservation, and using your equipment in an environmentally friendly way.

International Use

To meet international English language recommendations, some of the words you come across in this manual may look misspelled. The following is a list of these words in American English and their International counterparts.

American English	International Counterpart
Center	Centre
Meter	Metre
Gray	Grey
Aluminum	Aluminium

Throughout the manual, imperial measurements are listed first followed by the metric conversion. The following conversion units were used to convert the various measurements:

1 ATA (Atmospheres Absolute) = 14.7 psi (pounds per square inch)

1 ATA = 33 fsw (feet of sea water)

1 ATA = 10.33 metres of sea water

1 ATA = 1 bar

1 metre = 3.28 feet

$C° = (F° -32) ÷ 1.8$

1 kg (kilogram) = 2.2 lbs (pounds)

1 km (kilometre) = .621 miles

Note: For greater ease, many of the conversions in this text have been rounded to the nearest whole number, and may not reflect the exact conversion.

Serious Diving, Serious Fun

"I looked into the sea with the same sense of trespass that I have felt on every dive. A modest canyon opened below, full of dark green weeds, black sea urchins and small flower like white algae. Fingerlings browsed the scene. The sand sloped down into a clear, blue infinity. The sun struck so brightly I had to squint. My arms hanging at my sides, I kicked the fins languidly and traveled down, gaining speed, watching the beach reeling past. I stopped kicking and the momentum carried me on a fabulous glide."

— Jacques Cousteau
on his first scuba dive in 1943

Welcome to Your New Adventure!

Exploration, exotic locations, amazing color and beauty—these are just a few of the things you will experience in the spectacular underwater world. Welcome to your new adventure—innerspace. Congratulations! Scuba diving is a wonderful sport for everyone! You can look forward to many memorable diving adventures in the years to come.

We want you to know we appreciate your selection of the SSI Training Facility, which offers Scuba Schools International training aids and standards—the finest the scuba industry has to offer. You are an important new member of the worldwide SSI organization, and we want to do everything possible to help you love diving as much as we do.

Please read this brief introduction so you will know what to expect from your diving course. If you have any questions, your SSI Instructor is here to help.

The SSI Network

About Scuba Schools International

Scuba Schools International is a worldwide diver certification agency and educational support organization. Recognized as an innovative leader in diver education, we create state-of-the-art training programs, training standards and materials for all levels of diver education.

Our worldwide network is made up of five types of members.

SSI Delivers Quality

The SSI organization is set up to deliver quality. SSI Instructors can teach only at SSI Training Facilities, which are carefully screened to ensure they meet our standards.

SSI is the only organization in the industry with this level of quality control and accountability. This means you can have confidence in everyone associated with Scuba Schools International.

KNOWLEDGE · SKILLS · EQUIPMENT · EXPERIENCE

DIVER DIAMOND SSI

Divers

Certification gives you lifetime access to diving services, dive boats, diving activities and travel opportunities worldwide. Since certification is for life, it is the diver's responsibility to maintain proficiency with his or her knowledge and skills, keep his or her equipment serviced, and dive within the limits of his or her comfort and ability.

Instructors

SSI has certified tens of thousands of instructors worldwide. These instructors teach and certify divers through SSI Training Facilities. Instructors are responsible for meeting SSI Training Standards, using current materials and renewing their active status with SSI annually. Instructor performances are monitored by their training facilities.

Authorized Dealers

SSI Training Facilities include professional retailers, resorts, clubs and colleges all over the world. Training facilities operate a scuba diving school for diver and dive leader training; sell, rent and service high-quality equipment; sell compressed gas; and run trips, activities and boats for diving.

Regional Centres

SSI Regional Centres support Divers, Instructors and Training Facilities in key areas around the world. Their role is to:

◆ Ensure all Training Facilities meet SSI Standards.

◆ Certify Instructors to train divers.

◆ Distribute SSI products and produce certification cards.

◆ Implement a quality assurance system to enforce SSI Training Standards.

◆ Implement educational and business support programs to help their Training Facilities and Instructors be more successful and professional.

International Headquarters

International Headquarters writes SSI Training Standards and creates the skills and techniques for SSI courses. We produce educational materials and, with the help of our Regional Centres, translate them into many languages.

Serious Diving

There is a strong correlation between the quality of your training and the amount of fun you will have. To show you what is so special about learning to dive the "SSI way" we have highlighted some of the essential ingredients of your course.

KNOWLEDGE · SKILLS · EQUIPMENT · EXPERIENCE

DIVER DIAMOND
SSI
SCUBA SCHOOLS
INTERNATIONAL

What Every Diver Should Know

Decades of experience have taught us that there are four requirements to serious diving and serious fun.

Proper Knowledge

There are certain safety rules that must be learned. With a professional teaching system, you can study the information at your own pace. An instructor is always available for assistance.

Proper Skills

You must develop ability with basic scuba skills, such as moving in the water and equipment handling. The best way to learn is from a qualified instructor at a professional scuba school. Review and practice time reinforce the skills.

Proper Equipment

The most comfortable, convenient and enjoyable way to dive is with your own set of properly-fitted equipment. As you become familiar with your equipment, your ability level increases. Annual servicing assures your equipment's performance and minimizes malfunctions.

Proper Experience

While education helps develop knowledge and skills, the key to becoming a comfortable and confident diver is simply to dive as much as possible. Your experience and ability increase as you seek out different diving locations, meet new friends, have new adventures and explore new worlds. That is why SSI's motto is "Serious Diving, Serious Fun!"

SSI's Total Systems Approach

Scuba Schools International has developed three systems to help you acquire the proper knowledge, skills, equipment and experience for long-term diving.

Total Teaching System

Your Total Teaching System for the SSI Open Water Diver course includes a manual, study guide, video or DVD, dive tables and training record. This is a state-of-the-art programmed learning system that makes learning interesting and enjoyable.

Total Diving System

The Total Diving System includes all the equipment you need to explore the spectacular underwater world. Beginning in Section 1, you will be introduced to your Total Diving System. With personalized instruction from your SSI Instructor you will become comfortable and proficient with the equipment in your Total Diving System and the basic scuba skills.

Total DiveLog System

The SSI Total DiveLog System organizes every aspect of diving. First, it is your record of training. Second, it helps you plan dives and tracks your diving experiences. Third, it records your equipment purchases and servicing history. Fourth, it stores your certification cards, equipment warranty cards, airline tickets and trip itineraries. Over time it will become one of your most valuable possessions!

Getting Certified with SSI's 1-2-3 Approach

Scuba Schools International's 1-2-3 Approach is a natural learning progression with the goal of developing ability and comfort so you can really enjoy diving.

How Do SSI Students Get So Comfortable?

With SSI's exclusive water training method, Comfort Through Repetition, and personalized instruction from your SSI Instructor, you will experience the satisfaction of becoming comfortable and proficient with your equipment and scuba skills.

KNOWLEDGE · SKILLS
DIVER DIAMOND
SSI
EQUIPMENT · EXPERIENCE

Step 1 = Study Academics at Home

Start your adventure today with our top-rated home study program. At your convenience, and in the comfort of your own home, you review the text, watch a full-motion video or DVD, and complete a simple study guide.

To ensure you have met all the defined learning objectives, you will take a final exam. A passing score is 80%.

We want to make sure you are in good health for diving, so we require that you complete a confidential medical questionnaire. Developed by a committee of noted diving physicians, the questionnaire screens for certain medical conditions. If you have one of these conditions, it will be necessary for you to visit a physician.

Step 2 = Complete Academic Review & Pool Sessions

After your academic and equipment review session, it is off to the pool to become comfortable and proficient with your new scuba skills and equipment under the guidance of a professional SSI Instructor.

ACE Recommends SSI Courses

In the educational field, the American Council on Education (ACE) is the unifying voice for higher education in the United States. It represents all colleges and universities before the US federal government. ACE evaluates educational courses according to established college-level criteria and recommends college credit for those that measure up to these standards.

In 2001, ACE recommended four Scuba Schools International courses for college credit. To earn the recommendation, SSI had to pass an extensive ACE evaluative process conducted over several months. It culminated in an on-site visit to Scuba Schools International by ACE reviewers. The reviewers thoroughly examined SSI's teaching materials, our instructional process, our quality assurance system and other criteria.

The recommendation of SSI programs by the American Council on Education is an important symbol of quality you can trust because it comes from an unbiased third party.

KNOWLEDGE · SKILLS · DIVER DIAMOND · SSI · EQUIPMENT · EXPERIENCE

Step 3 = Complete Open Water Certification Dives

Let's go diving! You will join your Instructor for two exciting days of scuba diving. There you will apply all the knowledge and skills from steps 1 and 2. You can make the dives locally or join a scheduled trip to a diving destination. A referral can also be arranged if you already have a vacation planned.

SSI Quality Assurance

Did you know that someone at your Training Facility will personally monitor your instructor during your scuba course? That is right. A qualified person is responsible for making sure your instructor meets SSI Training Standards and that your course meets your satisfaction.

The advantages of on-site monitoring are obvious. It is proactive, rather than reactive. It is preventive; issues can be detected early and corrected quickly, before they become problems. Scuba Schools International is the only organization in the diving industry that has on-site monitors. This is possible because SSI Instructors are required to teach through an SSI Training Facility.

You should confirm with your Training Facility or your Regional Centre that your Instructor is active with Scuba Schools International.

Serious Fun: Diving is a Lifetime of Adventure!

After you are certified, you are ready to pursue a lifetime of adventure. Diving offers endless opportunities for exploration, discovery, education and new experiences. You can go as far as your passion and enthusiasm take you.

♦ **Explore the Waters in Your Backyard.**
No matter where you live, there are places full of adventure to dive. These dive sites are accessible and inexpensive. They allow you to gain experience and to use your knowledge, skills and equipment.

◆ **Explore the Waters of the World.** Travel to exotic lands and experience fascinating cultures. Seventy-two percent of the world is under water, and you have a license to explore it.

◆ **Join a Dive Club and Meet New Friends.** The best way to put your new knowledge, skills and equipment to practice is to meet other divers with experience. You can find out about local dive sites and vacation destinations. The only way to improve is to dive.

◆ **Become an "Underwater Photographer or Videographer."** The stunning beauty of the world underwater is a photographer's dream. With improvements in underwater photographic and video equipment, it is becoming progressively easier to get good results capturing your experiences and reproducing them for yourself, your family and friends.

◆ **Continue Your Education.** Your Open Water Diver certification is only the beginning of the SSI Educational System. SSI Specialty courses teach you specialized diving activities, and there are many courses to choose from. By combining specialties and experience you can earn SSI continuing educational ratings of Specialty, Advanced Open Water and Master Diver.

◆ **Become an SSI Dive Leader.** The Scuba Schools International worldwide network is constantly growing. To keep the SSI family strong, we always need new Dive Leaders. If you are interested in sharing the adventure of diving, please talk to your SSI Instructor about becoming an SSI Dive Leader.

However you choose to enjoy diving, your SSI Training Facility will be there to guide and assist you. Support them with your patronage and use them for the resource they are— your local link with the amazing world underwater.

Let's get started!

Your Diving Equipment

1

Air Delivery System
Regulator First-Stage
Regulator Second-Stage
Alternate Air Source
Cylinder

Snorkeling System
Mask
Snorkel
Fins

Buoyancy Control System
Buoyancy Compensator
Weights

Information System
Computer
Submersible Pressure Gauge
Compass

Exposure System
Wet Suit
Gloves (not shown)
Hood (not shown)
Boots

SECTION I

The Total Diving System

SCUBA SCHOOLS INTERNATIONAL

Every experienced diver understands that there is a definite link between owning your own equipment and being comfortable and confident in open water. To meet this goal, it is recommended that every diver own a high quality Total Diving System.

The Total Diving System is all the equipment you need to go diving, and something you may want to have for added enjoyment. For ease of understanding, we have divided it into seven subsystems. They are

1. **Snorkeling System**
2. **Exposure System**
3. **Air Delivery System**
4. **Information System**
5. **Total DiveLog System**
6. **Buoyancy Control System**
7. **Specialty Training and Accessory System**

Section I Objectives
After completing this section you will

◆ Be able to identify each subsystem and the equipment that make up each one,

◆ Be able to identify why we need each piece of equipment,

◆ Understand how to choose and fit Total Diving System elements to meet your personal diving needs and

◆ Understand the benefits of owning a personal Total Diving System.

The Snorkeling System

This is the first subsystem of the Total Diving System and the basic equipment used for snorkeling.

The first component of the Snorkeling System is the mask, your window to the underwater world.

The Mask

We need a mask because the human eye is not designed to work well when immersed in water. Vision is blurry, and the field of vision is limited. Since the eye is designed to see through air, which is less dense, and is much less dense than water, a mask is required to create an air pocket around the eye, simulating its natural environment.

Corrective Lenses

The diver whose vision needs correction has several options. The nearsighted diver may choose to correct vision with optical lenses measured in diopters — corrective lenses offered by manufacturers to replace stock lenses in particular mask models. Vision can also be corrected exactly by integrating prescription lenses into dive masks. Your prescription is produced by a qualified optical lab, and the lenses replace or are bonded to the faceplate of your mask. It is also possible to use contact lenses. All vision correction considerations and decisions should be made only with the consent and approval of your eye doctor and coordinated through your eye doctor and SSI Dealer.

The mask is one of the most important pieces of equipment you will ever purchase for diving.

There are two basic types of masks: the low volume and the high volume. The one you choose depends mostly on personal preference.

Low volume mask

Clear or colored silicone is the preferred material for diving masks. It is more durable than rubber, creates a soft, comfortable seal on your skin and allows light in for a more open feeling when the mask is on your face. Your instructor will teach you the proper care and maintenance procedure for your new mask.

High volume mask

Purge Valve

Some masks offer a one-way purge valve, which allows water inside to escape when the diver exhales into the mask through the nose. Some divers find it makes mask clearing easier and more convenient; however, you will learn how to comfortably clear any mask.

DIVER DIAMOND SSI

KNOWLEDGE · SKILLS · EQUIPMENT · EXPERIENCE

Mask Features

There are several important features to look for when choosing a mask. Your SSI Dealer and Instructor will help you choose the mask that is right for your face.

Mask Lens. The lens should be made of tempered glass. Mask lenses come from the factory with a film on them which needs to be cleaned off with a commercial mask cleaner before using an anti-fogging solution.

Frame. The frame should be made of a non-corrosive material such as hard plastic or stainless steel. Frameless masks should also be made of noncorrosive, durable materials.

Strap. The strap should adjust easily and lock in place. It should also be split at the back of the head or be wide enough to adhere to the head securely; a narrow, single band slips up and down too easily.

Comfort Strap

You may want to replace your strap with a comfort or neoprene strap. Many divers consider them to be more comfortable and easier to use.

Nose Pocket

Lens

Frame

Positive Locking Device

Strap

Positive Locking Device. Your mask should come equipped with a positive locking device which allows you to quickly adjust the mask strap and then lock it in place.

Nose Pockets. Nose or finger pockets built into masks are used for equalizing pressure inside the ears and sinuses as the diver descends and pressure increases. Equalization techniques are discussed in detail in Section 2.

Fitting the Mask

Facial contours differ, as do masks. The objective in finding a mask that fits is to match the mask skirt and your face. To check a mask for fit, tilt your head back and lay the mask on your face without using the strap. The force of gravity alone should keep a good fitting mask in place. Run a finger around the mask skirt to make sure the entire sealing edge touches your face and that no hair (including facial hair) is between the mask seal and your face. Then inhale gently through your nose to hold the mask against the face, tilt your head forward and look straight ahead. The mask should stay on with only a gentle inhalation, and you should not detect any air leak. Your SSI Dealer or Instructor will help you find the best fitting mask for you.

The Snorkel

The second component of the Snorkeling System is a snorkel. The reason we need a snorkel is so we do not have to constantly raise our heads above water to breathe while swimming, allowing for face down, relaxed exploration on the surface.

There are many options available when choosing a snorkel. The three main considerations are breathing, comfort and fit.

Snorkel Features

There are several features you may want to look for when selecting a snorkel. While these features may not affect the function of the snorkel, they will increase breathing comfort and fit.

Tube Style and Size. A snorkel will either have a solid or flexible tube design. The flexible snorkel is designed so that the snorkel hangs out of the way when using the scuba regulator. Solid tube snorkels should be contoured for proper positioning of the mouthpiece and to reduce drag in the water. Most manufacturers recommend a larger tube size for easier breathing.

Self-Draining Purge Valve. Some snorkels are equipped with a self-draining purge valve below the mouthpiece. Excess water is collected in a reservoir and effectively cleared from the snorkel with each exhalation, keeping the mouthpiece free of water.

Mouthpiece. Your snorkel should have a soft, comfortable mouthpiece that fits your mouth. The mouthpiece may also swivel so you can adjust it to the most comfortable position. Some snorkels are designed so the mouthpiece can be replaced.

Dry or Semi-dry Vent. Another added feature is a dry or semi-dry vent at the top of the snorkel. The dry or semi-dry vent helps prevent water on the surface from splashing into the snorkel tube and entering the mouthpiece, helping to keep water out and reducing, or eliminating the amount of water in the tube.

Dry or Semi-dry Vent

Mouthpiece

Solid and Flexible Tube Design

Self-Draining Purge Valve

Fins and Footwear

The third component of the Snorkeling System is the fins. The reason divers need fins is to help them move through the water efficiently. Fins are designed to maximize propulsion and minimize effort.

Fins come in two basic styles: the full-foot and the open-heel. Full-foot fins fit like shoes and come in standard sizes. Open-heel fins come in small, medium, large, and extra-large sizes and hold the foot in place with an adjustable heel strap. The open-heel fin and wet suit boot should be considered one unit and should be selected and fitted with one another.

Fin Features

Materials, designs, and features vary among fins, and, just as with the mask, you need to know these variations when choosing fins for your particular needs.

Which Fins?

The fin that is best suited for you will depend on your physical size, leg strength, environmental conditions and, most of all, comfort and fit. Your SSI Dealer or Instructor can assist you in finding the best possible fin for you.

DIVER DIAMOND
KNOWLEDGE • SKILLS • EXPERIENCE • EQUIPMENT
SSI
SCUBA SCHOOLS INTERNATIONAL

Materials. Fin blade materials include black rubber, polyurethane, thermoplastic, and various plastic composites. The type of materials used by the manufacturers will vary based on the design, performance and use of the fin. Many manufacturers use a combination of materials in order to accomplish multiple benefits.

Heel Strap

Blade

Buckle

Foot Well

Vent

Paddle Fin

Paddle, Vented and Split Fins. Manufacturers design fins for power efficiency and ease of use in the water. Your preference should depend on your physical size, leg strength, the type of diving you plan to do, environmental conditions and, of course, comfort and fit. An ideal design will give you the most amount of power with the least amount of energy.

Length and Flexibility. Choosing a particular blade strength and length is a personal decision. Larger, stiffer blades may provide more speed but may be harder to propel, and they would, therefore, be inappropriate for a diver who does not have the leg strength to use them for extended periods. Your SSI Dealer will help you find fins well suited to your experience level and physical capability.

Fitting the Fins

An open-heel fin with adjustable strap can compensate for slight variations in the size of the foot and wet suit boot because of expansion and contraction, and it can also permit the use of various thicknesses of boots. The open-heel and wet suit boot should be fitted together and be selected at the same time. Using a fin that fits well can prevent physical problems such as chafing and cramps and can also keep the fin from falling off. Though full-foot fins can be well fitted, they are not worn over wet suit boots so they are limited to use in comfortable temperatures. For extra comfort, the full-foot fin can be worn with a special sock of lycra or neoprene.

Split Fins

With open-heel fins, adjust the strap to keep the booted foot firmly in place. Then try to kick the fin off. It should stay on, and the foot pocket should neither bind, pinch, nor allow the foot too much excess movement. Also, the toes should not jam and overall fit should not restrict circulation.

Fin Satisfaction

The fins that will give you the most satisfaction will fit comfortably, feel good to use, not chafe with prolonged use and give you the most power with the least amount of effort. Your SSI Dealer or Instructor can help you make the right choice.

Though the full-foot fin is not adjustable and is usually not worn with a boot, the same rules of fit and comfort apply. To test the fit, stand and attempt to lift your heel out; it should stay snugly in place.

DIVER DIAMOND SSI

Snorkeling Vest

The ability to see, breathe and move are necessary elements of snorkeling; however, to enhance the enjoyment and comfort of these elements, the diver's buoyancy may be controlled by a buoyancy compensator, or BC. That is why the snorkeling vest, or BC, is the fourth component of the Snorkeling System.

The snorkeling vest, which fits like a bib, provides the snorkeler "lift" at the surface. The partially inflated vest minimizes water resistance for swimming, keeps the lungs slightly higher so that water pressure is lessened and breathing is easier and also helps keep the snorkel higher above the water surface. The diver adds or subtracts air, as needed, using an inflation tube or hose.

Snorkeling vests are also equipped with deflation mechanisms. Air is either allowed to escape slowly through the inflator hose or in some models, through a secondary dump valve.

Snorkeling vests should not be used for scuba diving. However, scuba diving buoyancy compensators (BCs) can be used for snorkeling. It is your decision whether to purchase a separate snorkeling vest for your future snorkeling experiences; however, some type of flotation device is highly recommended.

Mesh Snorkeling System Bag

The reason we need a mesh equipment bag is to keep the components of your Snorkeling System together and organized. Depending on the size, a mesh bag can hold as much or as little as you want and allows you to rinse your equipment in fresh water at the end of your diving day. Your SSI Dealer or Instructor can help you choose a mesh bag that fits your needs.

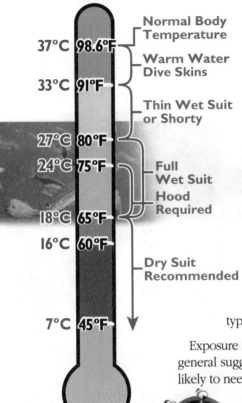

37°C 98.6°F — Normal Body Temperature

— Warm Water Dive Skins

33°C 91°F

— Thin Wet Suit or Shorty

27°C 80°F

24°C 75°F — Full Wet Suit

Hood Required

18°C 65°F

16°C 60°F

— Dry Suit Recommended

7°C 45°F

Exposure System

The second subsystem of the Total Diving System is the Exposure System. Just as we need appropriate clothing for varying temperatures on land, we also need appropriate protection for varying diving conditions.

The reason we need an exposure system when snorkeling and diving is because water absorbs body heat twenty-five times faster than air, so even warm water will "pull" heat from the body. Ideally, the normal body temperature of 98.6°F (37°C) should be maintained in water. Having fun and being comfortable under water start with staying warm. Your SSI Dealer or Instructor will help you choose the right Exposure System for the type of diving you will be experiencing.

Exposure suit needs are not exactly predictable. These are general suggestions about the type of exposure suit you are likely to need based on temperature ranges.

The amount of protection you use will depend ultimately on preference, except in colder waters where a dry suit is definitely necessary.

How Much Weight?

The amount of lead weight you will need will vary based on a number of things including the type, size and thickness of the suit you are using. This is because, typically, the thicker and larger the suit, the more buoyant it is.

We will first look at warm water dive skins, the favorite for snorkelers and warm water divers, and then go on to wet suits and dry suits which gradually increase in thermal protection.

DIVER DIAMOND SSI

Warm Water Dive Skins

At temperatures above 91°F (33°C), most divers will stay comfortable without protective wear. But even in the rare case of diving in water this warm, it is a good idea to be protected from sunburn, the marine environment and equipment that might cause chafing.

Dive skins are made from a variety of materials, some of which include lycra/nylon, polypropylene or neoprene. There are also bonded fabrics which are actually laminates of various fabrics. When combined, they create a warmer and better suit. Laminated fabrics may be warmer, more waterproof, more wind-proof, more breathable and more neutrally buoyant than other materials.

Wet Suits

Your body will still get wet while wearing a "wet" suit, but your body heat will pass through this extra layer of insulation much slower, keeping you warm longer. Wet suits are available as one-piece jumpsuits or as separate components in various styles and configurations.

Choosing a Wet Suit

The decisions you make regarding wet suits will involve variations in thickness and coverage. Thicknesses vary between one-half and seven millimetres. Coverage ranges from the limited protection of the wet suit vest, which only covers the torso, and the shorty, with its short arms, and legs, to a full-coverage wet suit, which can be made up of pants and jacket. Farmer Johns/Janes and jacket, or a one-piece jump suit, are also available. Most recreational diving is done in water temperatures between 50°F and 80°F (10°C and 27°C). Coverage and thickness preferences come into play at the extremes of this range, but it is generally agreed that full wet suits should be worn from 65° to 80°F

> ## Wet Suit Types
>
> Wet suits come in a wide range of styles for a variety of watersports. Obviously, divers require a wet suit made for underwater activities. Such wet suits are made of closed cell neoprene designed to keep you warm under water.
>
> DIVER DIAMOND
> SSI
> KNOWLEDGE • SKILLS • EQUIPMENT • EXPERIENCE

(18° to 24°C) and that a hood is required below 65°F (18°C). Gloves are important because of the increased exposure to cold water, cuts and abrasions while diving. Gloves are made of lycra fabrics, neoprene and combinations of these materials.

At extremely cold temperatures you can use a combination of wet suit components. Layering garments works as well under water as it does on land. A shorty or a jacket can be worn over a Farmer John, for instance. Movement becomes restricted, however, as you combine pieces or use thicker material.

Wet Suit Features

Some suits will feature zippers at the wrists, ankles, waist or up the sides. These make dressing easier but also allow more water to seep into the suit.

Other accessories added for convenience and comfort include pockets and knee and elbow pads. Spine pads conform to the diver's back and provide protection between the diver's back and the scuba cylinder, as well as lessen the exchange of water inside the suit. Some suits feature attached hoods which help prevent the leakage of water down the spine. Some wet suits have additional wrist and neck seals and can be termed "semi-dry" due to the way these seals effectively reduce the transfer of water in and out of the suit.

Wet Suit Fit

A good fit is one of the most important considerations when choosing a wet suit. If the suit is too loose, it will allow water to circulate inside it, cooling the body. If it is too tight, it can restrict circulation and movement, causing a diver to exert excess energy.

The suit should be snug without binding or pinching. It should not have gaps or sags under the arms or at the crotch. The neck, wrist, waist and ankle openings should be snug enough to prevent water from sloshing in, but loose enough to allow comfort and free blood circulation. Your SSI Dealer or Instructor will help you make sure you get the right fit.

Dry Suit Use

You may want to consider using a dry suit in waters below 65°F (18°C). Some divers prefer them at higher temperatures. This type of suit is used mainly in areas where the water is consistently colder.

Dry Suit

The dry suit provides complete protection against cold water. Unlike the wet suit, it keeps the body relatively dry. Dry suits can be made of neoprene, rubber, or laminated synthetic materials. An inflator hose from the first-stage regulator is attached to the suit so it can be inflated to compensate for compression as the diver descends and pressure increases. This prevents an uncomfortable suit squeeze and maintains the same degree of thermal protection regardless of depth.

It is recommended that if you dive in a dry suit, you participate in an SSI Dry Suit Specialty Course. Check with your SSI Dealer on the availability of a Dry Suit Specialty course.

Dry Suit

The Air Delivery System

The third subsystem of the Total Diving System is the Air Delivery System.

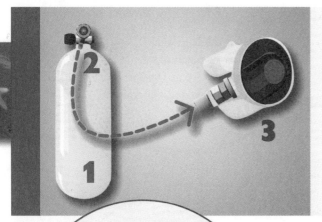

1. **CYLINDER:**
   Contains high-pressure filtered air.

2. **FIRST-STAGE REGULATOR:**
   Reduces high-pressure air to intermediate-pressure air.

3. **SECOND-STAGE REGULATOR:**
   Reduces intermediate-pressure air to breathable ambient pressure.

SCUBA

The regulator, combined with the cylinder system is what makes it possible for divers to breathe underwater untethered to the surface. The acronym SCUBA describes these two systems: **Self-Contained Underwater Breathing Apparatus.**

DIVER DIAMOND SSI

KNOWLEDGE · SKILLS · EQUIPMENT · EXPERIENCE

Air Delivery Systems have three components designed to work together to deliver air to the diver: the cylinder and the first-stage and second-stage regulators. The first-stage reduces the cylinder pressure to an intermediate pressure around 140 psi (10 bar) above ambient pressure (the pressure that surrounds you at any given depth). The air then travels through a hose to the second-stage regulator which is held in the diver's mouth. Here the air is essentially stopped and is available to the diver only on demand. When the diver inhales, the air pressure is reduced a second time to equal ambient pressure. Intermediate pressure is also used for BC and dry suit inflation.

The Cylinder

The cylinder is the foundation of the sport of scuba diving. The reason we need a cylinder is because it contains the air we breathe underwater. When combined with the regulator it forms the scuba unit (Self-Contained Underwater Breathing Apparatus), a self-contained air supply which enables the diver to remain under water untethered.

The cylinder is relatively simple in design. It is a seamless metal container capable of holding a large amount of breathing gas in its relatively small volume.

Choosing a Cylinder

When choosing a cylinder, realize that the size and construction material of the cylinder will affect your weighting and buoyancy under water.

Cylinders

Cylinders are regularly available for rent at dive stores, though you will know better what shape it is in and how well it has been maintained if you have your own. Also, having your own will enable you to become familiar with its weight and buoyancy characteristics.

Size. Cylinder sizes run anywhere from 6 to 190 cubic feet (340 to 5377 liters). The sizes most common to recreational diving are the 63 cu.ft. (1783 liters), 80 cu.ft. (2264 liters), 100 cu. ft. (2830 liters) and 120 cu. ft. (3396 liters). The steel 71.2 cu. ft. cylinder (2021 liters) is also common. Cylinders hold air at a maximum of between 2250 and 4400 pounds per square inch, or psi, (150 and 300 bar). They weigh around 30 to 40 pounds (13.6 to 18.1 kg) when empty, and since the weight of the air used is 5 to 10 pounds (2 to 4.5 kg), they can add 5 to 10 additional pounds of buoyancy at the end of the dive.

The O-ring

An important component of the cylinder valve is the O-ring. This small rubber or synthetic ring surrounds the air outlet and provides a seal between the cylinder and first-stage yoke. The O-ring is essential to the operation of the breathing system, so it is important to carry extras in case of excessive wear, breakage or loss.

Materials. Both steel and aluminium cylinders are subject to corrosion, but rust, which forms on the inside of steel cylinders, is destructive to the metal. Aluminium cylinders will affect your buoyancy more than steel because there is a greater weight difference between a full and an empty cylinder. Generally, they are negatively buoyant when full and positively buoyant when empty. Most steel cylinders are negatively buoyant and remain so throughout the dive.

Cylinder Valves

Cylinder valves are threaded and screwed into the cylinder at the top but are removed only when the cylinder is being inspected. Two commonly used valves are the K-valve and the DIN valve.

Burst Disk

K-valve

K-Valves. The most commonly used valve in the United States is the K-valve, which is used with the standard yoke first-stage connection. The K-valve has a simple on-off mechanism and is used in cylinders with up to 3000 psi (200 bar) working pressure.

A safety feature required of all cylinder valves is the burst disk. Air expands when heated, so a cylinder exposed to heat can become overpressurized. The burst disk prevents explosion by employing a thin metal or teflon disk which ruptures somewhere between 125 and 165 percent of a cylinder's stamped working pressure, thereby venting excess air in a controlled manner.

DIN-Valves. The DIN-valve, which stands for Deutsches Industrie Normen, is used on cylinders with a working pressure over 3000 psi (200 bar). While the DIN valve was originally used in Europe it has become popular in the United States, with U.S. manufacturers now designing and selling the valves. Regulator DIN conversion kits are also available which allow for removal of the standard regulator yoke connection and installation of the DIN screw-in connection. It is recommended that a DIN valve be installed by a certified technician. A DIN valve requires a DIN fitting on the first-stage of the regulator.

DIN-valve

Cylinder Features

Markings. Scuba cylinders must conform to government standards. In the United States, all cylinders have a set of markings stamped on the neck. Cylinders without the correct markings are illegal, and SSI Dealers will not fill cylinders which are not marked correctly.

TYPICAL ALUMINIUM CYLINDER MARKING DEFINITIONS

TC | 3ALM | 207BAR → Working | Cylinder Size in Cubic Feet

DOT | 3AL | 3000 | P417814 | LUXFER | 03△02 | S-80

Governmental Regulatory Agency | Material Specifications | Serial Number | Cylinder Manufacturer | Manufacturer Date & Logo

TYPICAL STEEL CYLINDER MARKING DEFINITIONS

Governmental Regulatory Agency | Exemption Number | Working | Date of Manufacture

© | DOT | E9791 | 3500 | TP5250 | 3-02

648652 | PST | 3☐02

Test Agency | Serial Number | Cylinder Manufacturer | Test | 1st Test Date & Logo

Cylinder Boots. The cylinder boot is a plastic or hard rubber cap which fits over the bottom of the cylinder. Boots serve two basic functions. They protect surfaces on which the cylinder is set and they allow the cylinder to stand upright while the diver assembles and disassembles the scuba unit. (It is recommended that the cylinder not be left standing upright when unattended.)

Some cylinder boots are enclosed, which can cause corrosion. Others have built-in drain vents.

← **Cylinder Boot**

Some boots are round and others are hex-shaped which helps prevent the cylinder from rolling.

The Regulator

Boyle's Law states that at a given temperature, pressure and volume are inversely proportional. What this means is that a diver 66 feet (20 metres) below sea level is under three times the amount of pressure and will need a regulator that can deliver three times the amount of gas (from the cylinder) to the diver's lungs easily and comfortably.

The Air Delivery System (the regulator and the cylinder) compensates for the changes in pressure, as described by Boyle, by supplying air, at surrounding (ambient) pressure, to the diver on demand when inhaling. Exhaled air is allowed to escape through an exhaust valve built into the second-stage. This is why a high quality Air Delivery System is a necessary part of the Total Diving System.

Depth Feet/Metres	ATM	Ambient Pressure PSI/bar	Volume of a Sealed Container	Density of Gas
0/0	1	14.7/1	1	1x
33/10	2	29.4/2	½	2x
66/20	3	44.1/3	⅓	3x
99/30	4	58.8/4	¼	4x

Boyle's Law

Choosing a Regulator

A primary consideration for the diver is how easily the regulator "breathes" at depth. Some work more smoothly than others and, therefore, cut down on breathing resistance.

Exertion, fatigue, depth, getting chilled, sharing air, and low cylinder pressure all create additional demand on the regulator and affect the ease of breathing. The regulator is designed to deliver air on demand. As the diver inhales, air is allowed to flow to the diver.

Easy Breathing

Regulators automatically adjust to increased pressure (ambient pressure) and deliver air to the diver on demand, via the second-stage, at a pressure equal to ambient pressure.

In order to make educated choices about regulators, you need a fundamental understanding of how they work.

The First-Stage

The first-stage regulator attaches to the cylinder. The purpose of the first-stage is twofold: reduce cylinder pressure to an intermediate pressure, and keep that pressure as constant as possible as the diver descends and ascends.

First-stage

The Second-Stage

The second-stage works similar to the first-stage but reduces intermediate hose pressure to a more breathable ambient level. Air from the hose passes into the second-stage through a small valve. Most all valve mechanisms manufactured today are designed to open with the flow of air (downstream valve). The downstream valve is very efficient and also best illustrates how the second-stage works. Inside of the second-stage is the diaphragm, which is the primary device that responds to inhalation and opens the valve to begin airflow to the lungs. When inhalation stops, the diaphragm returns to the closed position, halting airflow.

Second-stage

Regulator Evolution

Regulators have undergone evolution for many years. Improvements in design have made it easier than ever for the diver to breathe under water. Besides performance, the main differences you'll find in regulators are in the quality and durability of their components and materials, in their serviceability, and in their warranties.

The diaphragm also functions as a purge valve at the second-stage. By depressing the purge button on the outside of the mouthpiece with your fingers, the diaphragm is manually pushed inward. This allows air to enter the second-stage and clears water from inside the mouthpiece. It also vents off air before you remove the regulator from the cylinder.

Your SSI Dealer can help you select the best regulator for your particular needs and budget.

Alternate Air Sources

In addition to the primary second-stage, all scuba units should include a second air source for safety. This alternate air source comes into play in the unlikely event of the primary second-stage failing, or for any reason you and your buddy need to share air.

Alternate Second-Stage

There is no excuse for running out of air. Divers are equipped with a submersible pressure gauge to monitor their air supply. You should always plan to return to the surface with no less than 500 psi (34 bar) cylinder pressure remaining.

Emergency air sharing would then be initiated using this secondary source. Several design options are available.

The alternate second-stage simply utilizes two hoses and two second-stages, which are attached to the same first-stage.

Some alternate air sources are integrated into the BC. The inflator-integrated air source is an extra second-stage built right into the buoyancy compensator inflator hose or integrated into the power inflator mechanism on the inflator hose.

Redundant Breathing System

Another option is the independent, or redundant breathing system. This is a small reserve air cylinder with its own regulator and a supply sufficient for a return to the surface.

Information System

The Information System is the fourth subsystem of the Total Diving System. The reason we need an Information System is to monitor our life support systems and dive plan parametres (as planned in our Total DiveLog) while diving. Much like the gauges of a car, the Information System informs you how much air you have remaining, if you are going too deep or if you are ascending too fast. Various instruments allow you to monitor all these things, and help ensure you have an enjoyable experience. In later chapters, you will come to better understand the importance of having, and using, these valuable instruments.

Gauge Console

Various gauges can be separate but are also available in a console — a convenient housing which keeps several gauges together in one easily accessible source.

Dive Computer

The dive computer is more than an instrument. It is a data processor. The type and amount of information the dive computer processes vary between brands and styles.

Using a computer provides the diver with many advantages over conventional analog gauges and dive tables. Computer divers generally experience a significant increase in dive time.

Computer Features

All dive computers monitor depth and time while computing your theoretical nitrogen loading and unloading. Some also maintain a log of your dives in memory, which includes the dive number, maximum depth, maximum depth alarm, date, time, time remaining and total bottom time. Some incorporate the nitrogen loading bar graph, air consumption indicator, integrated cylinder pressure, an ascent rate monitor and alarm and even a thermometer and clock.

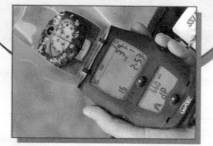

Hoseless Instruments

Hoseless instruments use a transmitter that sends a rapid frequency signal from the first-stage regulator to a receiver display unit which is usually worn on the wrist or attached to the BC.

They can accurately monitor and control their ascent rate, and the computer automates many routine tasks like tracking time between dives and logging essential information about the dives. Computers utilize a mathematical model that may vary from your personal physiology and, therefore, must be used properly and conservatively. Though basic training in dive computer theory and proper use is provided in this course, you will want to pursue your computer training and experience through your SSI Dealer's Continuing Education program.

Submersible Pressure Gauge (SPG)

The SPG is the diver's "fuel gauge." It is the instrument that tells the diver how much breathing gas remains in the scuba cylinder. The gauge attaches to a high pressure port on the first-stage of the regulator. Some things to look for include large markings and scratch resistant lenses. Gauges are available in Imperial and metric units and are digital as well as analog. The SPG should be monitored frequently throughout the dive.

Submersible Pressure Guage

Depth Gauge

Knowing your depth is important in adhering to your dive plan. You need to know when you have reached a targeted depth, and you need to monitor your current depth to ensure that planned limits are not exceeded. Most analog depth gauges are calibrated at feet sea water (FSW) and some are equipped with a maximum depth indicator which records the deepest point reached during a dive. Some analog depth gauges also have altitude compensation.

Digital gauges are more accurate than analog gauges and are standard in all dive computers.

Depth Gauge

Timing Device

The most prevalent of the timing devices is the dive computer. The dive watch is also available as a timing device. The watch, of course, tells time, but it also helps the diver keep track of the time elapsing during a dive. A one-way bezel around the perimeter of the watch face is set at the start of the dive to indicate how many minutes the actual dive has been under way. Digital watches show time and elapsing time automatically with continuous readouts.

Another timing device is the dive timer. This instrument is automatically activated by pressure as the diver descends, and it stops when the diver returns to the surface, thus showing the total time a diver has spent under water. Dive timers keep track of time spent on the surface between dives as well. Watches should be rated to a depth of at least 100 metres, and better yet, 20 ATMs. Digital timing devices are a standard feature of dive computers and automatically record dive total times.

Compass

The compass helps the diver maintain a sense of direction when natural navigation is not possible due to a lack of distinct underwater features or low visibility. It also indicates the way back to an original dive point. There are several styles of compasses.

Side-Reading Compass

Side-Reading Compass. This compass either attaches to the wrist or fits in the gauge console and can be read from the top or the side.

Top-Reading Compass

Top-Reading Navigational Compass. This compass is designed to plot course headings accurately and to aid in return navigation. It also fits either on the wrist or in a console.

Digital Compass. Digital compasses provide more detailed information than standard compasses; however, they require a power source, such as a battery. Digital compasses have many beneficial features for different types of diving. Consult your SSI Dealer for more information.

Digital Compass

Note: Certain metals can alter the indicated direction of the compass. Use caution when using a compass and diving near wrecks and heavy mineral deposits.

You will only get an introduction to navigation in this course. However, SSI Navigation Specialty Courses with detailed information on compass use and navigation techniques are offered by your SSI Dealer.

Thermometers

The thermometer is another valuable piece of equipment in recording dives. You can record temperatures at particular dive sites so that variations in features (algae, visibility) affected by temperature or your exposure suit needs can be predicted. Many new digital gauges and dive computers come with a built-in thermometer.

Information System Configurations

Information System configurations come in a variety of styles and colors to choose from; however, there are three main information system configurations that you are likely to encounter.

System Configuration 1. This configuration consists of an air integrated computer and a digital or standard compass. It provides you with the best possible information and is the ideal choice for divers who want all of their dive information at a glance.

System 1

System Configuration 2. The second configuration consists of a non-air integrated computer, analog SPG, and a digital or standard compass. It is the most common information system configuration. It does not offer the benefit of integrated air computations, but it offers all the other major benefits of computer diving.

System Configuration 3. This is the most traditional system configurations. It is made of all analog gauges, with or without a compass. Very few people dive with this configuration anymore due to the ease of use and the relatively low cost of dive computers.

System 2

System 3

The Total SSI DiveLog System

Having the equipment is only the beginning. Planning your dives requires the SSI Total DiveLog System, the fifth subsystem of the Total Diving System.

A key function of the SSI DiveLog is to track your continuing education and your number of logged dives. Both are valuable and rewarded with the SSI Recognition System. All your logged dives count toward Continuing Education ratings, such as Specialty Divers, Advanced Open Water Diver and Master Diver, plus you can receive recognition stickers and cards just for logging dives.

Recognition Cards

Work towards your Century Diver, Gold500 Diver, Platinum1000 Diver or Platinum Pro5000 Diver cards. These prestigious cards were the first in the industry to recognize diving skills you develop and experience you gain as you log dives.

Buoyancy Control System

The Buoyancy Compensator

Over-expansion Relief Valve

Dump Valve

Inflator Hose

LPI (Low-Pressure Inflator)

Adjustment Strap

Oral Inflator

Buckle

The sixth subsystem of the Total Diving System is the Buoyancy Control System. As you will learn, the Buoyancy Control System makes ascending, descending, neutral buoyancy and surface floatation quite easy. However, to understand why you need a BC you must first understand Archimedes' Principle, which states that an object (diver) is buoyed up by a force equal to the weight of the water it displaces. As a diver adds air to the BC, it expands, displacing more water. Therefore, the buoyant force increases causing a diver to rise underwater, or to float higher on the surface.

The scuba diver's Buoyancy Compensator, or BC, balances factors that play a role in Archimedes' Principle. Such factors are body weight, various bodies' tendencies toward positive or negative buoyancy, the type of Exposure System you are using and the relative weight of other equipment being used in order to maintain neutral buoyancy under water. Keep in mind that each time you change or vary your Exposure System and equipment configuration, your buoyancy characteristics will also change.

Like the snorkeler's vest, the BC can also be, and should be, inflated at the surface, allowing the diver to float and move around without expending energy. In scuba this is valuable for moving to and from dive sites and surveying dive locations from the surface.

Buoyancy Control System Features

Low-Pressure Inflator

Inflators. All BCs are equipped to accommodate an inflator mechanism. The inflator mechanism can inflate the BC both orally and mechanically. Oral inflators consist of a manual control button which opens an air passage through a hose connected to the BC. The button is depressed and the diver blows into a mouthpiece located in the inflation mechanism. Power inflators allow you to inflate the BC (at the push of a button) with air from the cylinder. Cylinder air is reduced to a low pressure by design, hence the name low-pressure inflator.

Deflators. BCs are deflated in one of two ways. The air can be released slowly by pushing the manual control button on the inflator mechanism, or it can be released quickly through a dump valve. Dump valves are activated by a pull string, lever or a release which is controlled by the diver.

Manual Control Button

When using the manual control button, extend the inflator hose to the highest point in order to get the greatest efficiency in deflation.

A safety feature built into BCs is the overexpansion relief valve which is designed to let air vent off when the BC overexpands. Many BCs have a dump valve located in three different places to allow you to dump air in various positions.

Overexpansion Relief Valve

Inflator-Integrated Air Source. Another feature is an alternate breathing apparatus combined with the inflator assembly. This type of alternate air source can eliminate one low pressure hose from the system and replace the conventional alternate regulator.

Inflator-Integrated Air

Integrated Weight System. An alternative to the traditional weight belt is the integrated weight system which is built into specially equipped buoyancy compensators. These built-in weight systems offer the advantage by moving the weight from your hips to the BC, and they may help reduce back stress.

BC-Integrated Weights

For safety reasons, divers using integrated weights must learn how to detach the weights quickly. Also, make sure that your buddy becomes familiar with their operation. This can be learned safely by practicing in confined water or a pool.

See your SSI Training Facility and your manufacturer's instructions for more information on releasing the weight system.

Lift. The amount of lift, or how much weight the BC can support at the surface, is determined by the volume of air the BC will hold. This means that warm-water, low-profile BCs, while comfortable, may not provide adequate lift when diving (with heavy weights and equipment) in cold waters. Conversely, some BCs, meant to provide a great amount of lift, may be bulkier and less comfortable than the warm water diver wants.

Choose a BC that has sufficient lift for your body weight. Most manufacturers list the amount of lift each style of BC is designed to provide.

Buckles, Belts, and Straps

Other Features. Most BCs include pockets, several buckles, belts and straps both for utility, convenience and adjustment. A wide cummerbund replaces a standard waist belt on some models, compensating for wet suit compression and expansion and reducing up and down movement of the cylinder.

The cylinder retaining band is an adjustable nylon strap which buckles to the air cylinder holding it firmly in place, and it can be easily adjusted to accommodate cylinders of varying diameters.

On most models, velcro straps, buckles and other attachments are used to streamline equipment by attaching hoses, lights, instruments, etc., to the BC. Trim all these items as best as you can with the equipment you are using.

The BC you choose will depend mostly on personal comfort and preference, and the type of environment in which you do most of your diving. Work with your local SSI Dealer or Instructor to determine the BC that best suits you.

Proper Weighting

Added weight, whether from a weight belt or weight integrated BC, counteracts the positive buoyancy of the diver's body and exposure suit on the surface, providing slightly negative buoyancy which allows the diver to descend.

Belts. The most common material used for the belt is webbed nylon. It is durable and can support plenty of weight. A variation on the nylon belt is one which includes a flexible depth compensating device which shrinks as the exposure suit compresses. A design which combines practicality and comfort is the pocket weight belt, which is made from both neoprene and nylon mesh. This design uses internal weight pockets to eliminate the bulk and discomfort of exposed weights. With weight pockets, weights also can be added or subtracted easily while the belt is being worn.

Buckles. The buckle of the belt should be made of a non-corrosive material and should be able to be opened with one hand for quick release.

Weights. Lead weights come in a variety of sizes, shapes and weight values. Some lead weights feature vinyl coatings, available in colors, which protect boat and pool

Buoyancy Control

As the diver descends, increasing pressure compresses the exposure suit, eliminating some of its buoyancy while the weight system remains at a constant weight, so air is added to the BC to counteract the loss of buoyancy. On ascent, air must be vented from the BC to control the rate of ascent. Air may also need to be released if your cylinder becomes buoyant due to air consumption.

DIVER DIAMOND **SSI** SCUBA SCHOOLS INTERNATIONAL

KNOWLEDGE • SKILLS • EQUIPMENT • EXPERIENCE

Weight Belts

decks from scratches. Another design is the soft weight, consisting of a sealed pouch full of lead shot. These pouches are available in various weight sizes and are used with pocket weight belts and weight integrated BCs. Some consider shot-filled weights to be more comfortable because they can conform to the body and more environmentally friendly should the weights be dropped or come loose while diving.

Choosing Your Weighting

Some determinations regarding the added weight can be made on land, but the most important determination — exactly how much weight you need relative to your body and equipment — can be made only in the water. Other choices when selecting added weight or a weight belt include the material in the belt and various weight designs.

Proper Weighting

If you are using a weight belt (not a weight integrated BC), it should be adjusted to fit snugly, with the weights distributed evenly and positioned near the front of the hips. The buckle is positioned to open opposite of the BC strap buckle. In other words, adjust the buckles so that they open from opposite sides — the weight belt with right hand release and the BC with left hand release, or vice versa. The reason for this is that the two should never be confused.

To fit your belt or weight integrated BC with the proper amount of weight, first get

Weight Ditching

Weight ditching is a very important skill, and you and your buddy need to know how to remove your own as well as each other's weight quickly.

DIVER DIAMOND SSI
SCUBA SCHOOLS INTERNATIONAL
KNOWLEDGE · SKILLS · EXPERIENCE · EQUIPMENT

1

in confined water while wearing all the other equipment. Move to a place where you can float, then with your vest deflated, add enough weight to make yourself neutrally buoyant. You will neither sink nor float, and your eyes will rise to about water level when you inhale and sink slightly below the surface when you exhale.

Specialty Training and Accessory System

The seventh subsystem of the Total Diving System is the Specialty Training and Accessory System. The equipment covered so far consists of the basics. When you know how to use them, you will essentially know how to dive. In addition to the basics, there are some accessories which can further help you become a more comfortable and confident diver.

Diver's Luggage

Diver's Luggage is often the most important piece of equipment when it comes to the protection of your Total Diving System. The following diver's luggage features are recommended for maximal protection of your equipment:

Size. Your diver's luggage should be large enough to carry all your dive equipment, with the exception of your regulator, which you may want to pack and carry separately.

Durable and Versatile. Your diver's luggage should be very durable to withstand the rigors of travel but easy to roll and carry. It should be made of mildew resistant fabric and have compartments for easy organization.

Locking Device. Your diver's luggage should be designed so each compartment can be locked and remain locked while traveling.

Wheels. Wheels are available on most full-size diver's luggage for ease of movement during travel and should be considered a necessity. The wheels should be made from a durable material that will not break, under heavy loads, or rust from contact with moisture.

Consult your SSI Dealer for more information about diver's luggage.

Flags and Floats

It is hard for boaters to see divers on the surface, and it would be impossible for boaters to know when divers are under them if not for a system of communicating these facts. The diver's flag and dive boat flag serve this purpose. However, caution must still be exercised because some boaters are unaware of the meaning of the diver's flags.

The two kinds of flags used are the recreational diver's flag and the alpha flag, or the international "diver down" flag. The recreational diver's flag is red with a diagonal white stripe. It says, "There are divers below; keep clear and travel at slow speed." It is flown only when divers are actually in the water. The recreational diver's flag is governed by tradition, and in some places, by law. Your SSI Dealer will know the rules in your area.

Recreational Divers Flag

Diver's flags are displayed on some sort of float. This could be a buoy, inner tube, surfboard or small raft. Larger rafts and boats make good floats in deep water situations or on repetitive dives because you can store equipment in them or use them in emergencies.

The alpha flag is blue and white with a "V" cut into one side. It is flown from boats and says, "This vessel has divers below and maneuverability is restricted." It is often used during commercial dives when divers are tethered to the boat by hoses or lines. The alpha flag is the dominant flag used in international and inland navigable waterways.

Alpha Flag

Signaling Devices

Signaling devices are used to attract attention to yourself on the surface or under water. They are used because they work much better than shouting, they can be more easily seen or heard over the waves and wind and they take less energy. Also, some signaling devices are specifically designed for use under water. They may also be used as a routine part of a dive plan, such as inflatable surface markers, described below or to alert a boat, the shore or your buddy in the event of an emergency.

Whistles and Alarms. Plastic whistles and other audible signaling devices such as alarms work well for signaling on the surface. Attach them to your BC inflator hose or another easily accessible place.

Signal Flares. The day/night flare can be used to signal an emergency, or to communicate a diver's whereabouts to a boat crew or a party on shore. The red flare is for emergencies, and the white flare is for location.

Inflatable Surface Marker. Surface markers that fit into your BC pocket are available and can be inflated on the surface orally or with your second-stage. These devices extend 4 or more feet (1.2 metres) above the water so you can attract attention on the surface.

Underwater Audible Devices. There are a variety of devices on the market that make noise under water to attract your buddy's attention. These devices vary from a plastic ball that bangs on your cylinder, to sophisticated alarms. Your SSI Dealer has various types of underwater signaling devices available. They can help you choose which ones are right for you.

Surface Markers Required

Many live-aboard dive boats and dive boat operators now require that each diver have and use inflatable surface markers so that they can be more easily seen on the surface for pickup after a dive.

DIVER DIAMOND
KNOWLEDGE · SKILLS · EQUIPMENT · EXPERIENCE
SSI SCUBA SCHOOLS INTERNATIONAL

Save-a-Dive System

It would be a shame to have to call off a dive because of something as simple as a broken mask strap. A small kit containing essential spare parts and some basic tools such as pliers, crescent wrench, allen wrenches, and a screw driver should always be taken along. Make certain that the items you carry are appropriate replacement parts for your specific pieces of diving equipment. Mask and fin straps are not necessarily generic. See your SSI Dealer for consultation. At a minimum, it is recommended to include the following in your Save-a-Dive System:

Fin Straps and Buckles

Mask Straps and Buckles

Snorkel Keeper

Knife Retaining Kit

Knife Strap and Buckles

Needle and Thread

Various O-Rings

Batteries for Lights and Cameras

Weight Belt and Buckle

Screwdrivers (Standard and Phillips)

Pliers

Anti-Fogging Solution

Tie Wraps

Dust Cap

First-Stage Intermediate Port Plug

First-Stage High Pressure Port Plug

Silicone Spray

FDA Approved Silicone

Exposure Suit Cement

BC Patch Kit

BC Buckles

Crescent Wrench

Allen Wrenches

Second-Stage Mouthpiece

First Aid Kit

When traveling it is recommended you carry an extra mask and extra high and low pressure hoses. Other items you might consider have to do with your personal equipment, such as a camera system. An SSI Equipment Techniques Specialty will teach you more about your equipment and field repairs.

Underwater Lights

Water absorbs light, which affects the colors you see under water. Different colors of the spectrum are absorbed at different depths depending on the wavelength of the color. Low frequency reds are absorbed first, while high frequency blues and greys travel further in the water column. The mnemonic ROY G. BIV (Red, Orange, Yellow, Green, Blue, Indigo, Violet) can be used to remember the order in which the colors are absorbed, from shallow to deep water. It is highly recommended to bring artificial light (an underwater light) with you on dives, even during the day, to restore the color under water.

10'-15' (3-4.5 metres) – Red

30' (9 metres) – Orange

60' (18 metres) – Yellow

90'-150' (27-46 metres) – Green

150' (46 metres) – Blue

150' + (46+ metres) – Indigo, Violet

In clear water, approximate depths of color absorption

Using a light, even during the day, allows you to enjoy the "true" vibrant colors the reef has to offer.

The most common device is the underwater light, powered by either rechargeable or replaceable batteries. These are waterproof flashlights with varying degrees of durability and candle power.

Rechargeable lights may cost more initially, but eliminate the need to buy and dispose of batteries, saving you money and protecting the environment. You must remember to recharge the batteries after use and consider carrying power adapters when traveling abroad. Follow manufacturer's recommendations for recharging. Lights come in a variety of sizes from the personal locator light, which attaches to the cylinder valve or to the diver, to narrow beam and wide beam flashlights. More information on lights can be obtained from your SSI Dealer.

When you complete your SSI Night Diving Specialty, you will have a better understanding of the differences between night and day diving.

Chemical Glow Light. It is constructed of a small glass inner tube containing one chemical and a larger plastic outer tube containing another. When you bend the plastic tube, the tube inside breaks and the chemicals mix, creating a bright glow. The light usually attaches to the diver's cylinder valve or to the diver as a way for buddies to keep track of each other at night or in limited visibility. However, they should not be used instead of a light or as a back-up light. After use, the lights should be properly discarded and not left in the water or on the shore. Make sure that local laws or rules allow you to use chemical glow lights when diving.

Battery Powered Glow Light. Battery powered glow lights are becoming more and more commonplace as they reduce the amount of waste created by chemical glow lights and are inexpensive to purchase. These lights come in a variety of colors and configurations and will last a very long time with proper maintenance and care.

Diver's Tool

The diver's tool is very handy. Most commonly the tool fits into a sheath attached at an easily accessible place, such as on the BC. It can be used to free yourself if you become ensnared while under water and to tap on your cylinder to get a buddy's attention. The tool should be made of non-corrosive metal and should be strong and sharp. Make sure that local laws or rules allow you to have and carry a dive tool when diving.

Tool Construction

It is recommended that the metal of the tool extend all the way through the handle.

DIVER DIAMOND
SSI
KNOWLEDGE • SKILLS • EXPERIENCE • EQUIPMENT

Maintaining Your Total Diving System

Buoyancy Compensator

After the dive, drain the BC of any water that has entered through the inflator hose. Then rinse the BC inside and out with clean, fresh water. To rinse the inside, fill it about one-third with water through the inflator hose. Then inflate it and slosh the water around. It is recommended that you drain the water through an exhaust valve. If this is not possible, you may need to drain the water by inverting the BC and holding the inflator hose down with the oral inflator open. Make sure push buttons and inflator components are clean and clear of silt or impurities. BCs drain best when they are fully inflated.

When storing the BC, allow it to dry in an open area, and leave it half full of air to keep the insides from sticking together.

You can check for leaks in the BC by filling it with air and submersing it in a bathtub while watching for bubbles. If it does leak, it should be taken to your SSI Dealer for professional repair. Check with your owner's manual to see how often your BC should be serviced.

Regulator

Make sure the dust cap is clean and dry before replacing it. Flush the mouthpiece and exhaust port with clean, fresh water. It is important not to let any water into the hoses. To avoid water contamination of the inside of the hoses, never push the purge valve while rinsing the inside of the second-stage.

Do not hang the regulator by the hose when storing. This can permanently bend the hose and weaken it at the point of the bend.

Gently wind the hoses into a storage bag to prevent damage and keep out dust. Hose protectors can be added where the hose meets the first-stage of your regulator to protect your hoses from excess wear.

All repairs to the regulator should be done by your SSI Dealer, and it is recommended to have them serviced annually, or as often as is required by your owner's manual. Record maintenance of your scuba equipment in the Equipment section of your SSI Total DiveLog.

Information System

As with the Air Delivery System, rinse the Information System and store it clean and dry. Do not allow water inside the hose, and when storing, do not hang it by the hose. Check your owner's manual to see how often it recommends that you have your instruments serviced. You will also need to periodically have the batteries in digital instruments changed. Many digital instruments can only be serviced by the manufacturer. This may also include replacement of the batteries. It is impossible to purchase some of these specialized batteries in remote dive destinations. Periodic accuracy checks can be done at your SSI Dealer.

Cylinder

The safe and efficient operation of the cylinder depends on proper maintenance and inspection. Like any other piece of equipment, it should be kept clean and dry, but there are additional, specific steps you must take in order to keep the cylinder safe and working properly.

Storing and Transporting the Cylinder. Never store a cylinder empty. It is recommended that some air pressure remain in the cylinder. This will prevent moisture from getting in, or condensing due to temperature changes. It is recommended that cylinders be stored lying down whenever possible.

Any time a cylinder is stored, it should be well secured and kept away from children.

Secure the cylinder during transport in an automobile by laying it down lengthwise (with the valve end toward the rear) on the floor, trunk, or truck bed. Wrap the valve with thick padding and tie the cylinder down or block it so that it cannot easily move, even if jolted. Also, keep it out of direct sunlight and avoid prolonged storage in a place which may overheat.

Preventing Damage to the Cylinder. Prevent interior moisture and contamination by making certain that cylinder fittings, openings and O-rings are dry before system assembly. There are some precautions you can take periodically to make sure your cylinder is dry and uncontaminated inside. Follow the rule of "look and feel, smell, and listen":

Look and Feel. Turn the valve on and watch the air as it comes out. Damp air is white. Dry air is invisible. Also, feel the stream of air, and rub your fingers to see if any moisture has escaped the cylinder.

Smell. If the air smells damp or metallic, there could be water, oil, or rust inside. Pure air does not have any odor.

Listen. While turning the cylinder upside-down, listen for loose particles and water. Any rattling could signal that there are rust chips or other impurities inside. If you suspect anything, take the cylinder to your SSI Dealer for a professional VIP® inspection.

VIP® (Visual Inspection Program). Always have a V.I.P.® done at least once a year, or more frequently with heavy use, by your SSI Dealer. This visual inspection will determine whether there is any contamination inside and will assess the general condition of the cylinder. The inspection starts with looking the cylinder over for obvious flaws such as dents or stripped threads, then checking the interior for contaminants or corrosion.

Hydrostatic Testing. In the United States, a cylinder must be hydrostatically tested every five years. In other countries this varies and can be as frequent as every year. The hydrotester must be licensed and have current authorization from the proper governmental control agency. The hydrostatic test measures the elasticity of the cylinder's metal chamber. If the tolerance is exceeded, the metal of the cylinder is considered fatigued, and the cylinder must be condemned.

A cylinder that fails a hydro-test could pass a second test because it has already been expanded. In this case a second opinion could be misleading. The cylinder is condemned after failing a hydro-test and must not be used again.

The SSI Equipment Service Program

The Equipment Service Program, which is available through your SSI Dealer, is a complete maintenance program designed to keep the components of your Total Diving System performing to the best of their potential. Below is an explanation of each of the services that make up the SSI Equipment Service Program.

Air Delivery System Protection

Regulators are totally disassembled and cleaned in a special cleaning solution. High-pressure and low-pressure seats are replaced along with all dynamic o-rings, exhaust valves, and high pressure filters. Performance tests are conducted to manufacturer warranty specifications.

Nitrox Air Delivery System Protection

This is the same as Air Delivery System Protection, but is performed on Nitrox equipment. A green Nitrox hose sleeve is used to mark your Nitrox Air Delivery System rather than a yellow hose sleeve.

Information System Protection

Submersible pressure gauges, depth gauges, pressure activated dive timers, and dive computers are checked for accuracy in a pressure vessel, and the indicated readings versus true readings are noted.

Buoyancy Control System Protection

Buoyancy compensators are inspected for leaks, buckle strap tension and bladder seam integrity. Inflator mechanisms are disassembled, cleaned and rebuilt, the inner bladder rinsed with B.C. conditioner and over-pressure release valves are cleaned and tested for proper operation, all to manufacturer warranty specifications.

Visual Inspection Protection (and Visual Plus®)

Annually, cylinders are inspected internally and externally for rust, corrosion and cracks to the standards of DOT and CGA. It is suggested that aluminium cylinders be tested with Visual Plus to ensure the integrity and strength of the neck and threads.

Exposure System Protection

Services are available for exposure suits (wet and dry). Minor repairs are done in house and alterations are done with the original manufacturer.

When you have your equipment serviced or repaired, take along your SSI Total DiveLog so the technician can record the service. This will be valuable should you decide to upgrade your equipment someday.

Summary

Diving is an enjoyable activity once you begin to get comfortable with the necessary techniques and equipment. We stated earlier that "ability equals comfort, and comfort equals enjoyment." The better you become at handling and making proper use of the equipment, the more comfortable you will become as a diver.

Work with your local SSI Dealer and Instructor in determining your needs, and acquire your own equipment as soon as you can. We recommend that you purchase a Total Diving System while still in training so you can use your equipment under the supervision of your Instructor. You will also be much more comfortable when you do your open water dives.

Once you have your equipment, your SSI Dealer will also help you maintain, inspect, repair and fill your air cylinder. Also see your dealer about new developments in equipment, and the proper techniques for using new items. This will be especially necessary as you progress into advanced courses that depend on equipment, such as computer diving and dry suit diving. Your SSI Dealer and Instructor are equipment experts. Consult them any time you have questions or need advice on purchasing or maintaining equipment.

Get to know your equipment, practice with it, keep it clean and well organized. When using your equipment starts to become second nature, your enjoyment of recreational diving will really take off. Soon you will be diving right along with the other welcome members of the diving community.

Section I Study Guide Questions

1. _____ _____ built into masks are used for equalizing pressure in the ears and sinuses.

2. The fin that is best suited for you will depend on your physical size, leg strength, environmental conditions and, most of all, _____ and _____.

3. Water absorbs body heat _____ times faster than air.

4. The amount of lead weight you will need will vary based on a number of things including the type, size and _____ of the suit you are using.

5. Most recreational diving is done in temperatures between about 50° F - 80° F (10° C- 27° C). Coverage and thickness preferences come into play at the warm and cold extremes of this range, but it is generally agreed that full wet suits should be worn from _____ .

6. A _____ _____ is one of the most important considerations when choosing a wet suit.

7. You may want to consider using a _____ _____ in waters below 65° F (16° C).

8. The acronym S.C.U.B.A. stands for _____
_____ _____
_____ _____ .

9. _____ cylinders will affect your buoyancy more than _____, because there is a greater weight difference between a full and empty cylinder.

10. Boyle's Law

Depth Feet/Metres	ATM	PSI/Bar Ambient Pressure	Volume of a Sealed Container	Density of Gas
0/0	1	14.7/1	1	D
33/10	2	B	1/2	2x
66/20	3	44.1/3	C	3x
A	4	58.8/4	1/4	4x

Circle the correct combination.

a) A = 88/27, B = 29.4/2, C = 2/3, D= 6x

b) A = 99/30, B = 29.4/2, C = 1/3, D = 1x

c) A = 92/30, B= 33.8/2, C= 1/3, D= 8x

d) A = 99/30, B= 30.4/2, C= 1/8, D= .5x

11. There is no excuse for running out of air. Divers are equipped with a _____ _____ _____ to monitor their air supply.

12. Using a _____ provides the diver with many advantages over conventional analog gauges and dive tables.

13. The _____ helps the diver maintain a sense of direction when natural navigation is not possible due to lack of distinct underwater features or low visibility.

1

14. When using the manual control button, extend the
_____ _____ to the highest point in
order to get the greatest efficiency in deflation.

15. Diver's Luggage is often the most important piece of equipment when
it comes to the protection of your _____
_____ _____ .

16. The two kinds of flags used are the _____
diver's flag and the _____ flag, or the international "diver
down" flag.

17. Many live-aboard dive boats and dive boat operators now require that
each diver have and use _____
_____ _____ so that they can be
more easily seen on the surface for pickup after the dive.

18. When traveling it is recommended to carry an extra _____ ,
and extra _____ and _____ pressure hoses.

19. In the U.S. a cylinder must be hydrostatically tested every _____
_____ and visually inspected every _____ .

20. Work with your local SSI Dealer and Instructor in determining your
needs, and acquire your own _____ as soon
as you can.

Using Your Diving Equipment

SECTION 2

One must learn by doing the thing;
though you think you know it;
you can't be certain until you try.

— Sophocles

You have already taken an important step in your training as a diver by getting to know the pieces of equipment you will be utilizing when you get in the water. Now to further prepare you, we will cover some basic skills you need to begin mastering. These skills are not difficult and are very important. First of all, you need to know how to use the equipment in order to know how to dive; equipment and skills are inseparable. Plus, knowing these skills will reduce your apprehension about being in open water for the first time, and practicing them will make all the difference in becoming a comfortable and confident diver.

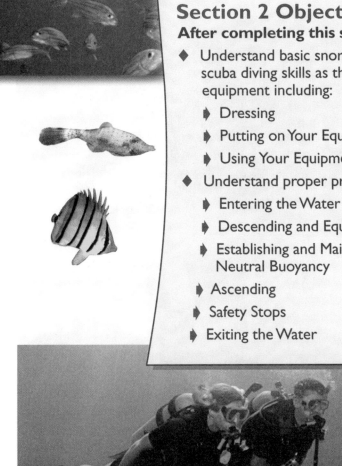

Section 2 Objectives
After completing this section you will

◆ Understand basic snorkeling and scuba diving skills as they relate to your equipment including:

  ▶ Dressing

  ▶ Putting on Your Equipment

  ▶ Using Your Equipment

◆ Understand proper procedures for:

  ▶ Entering the Water

  ▶ Descending and Equalizing Pressure

  ▶ Establishing and Maintaining Neutral Buoyancy

  ▶ Ascending

  ▶ Safety Stops

  ▶ Exiting the Water

The Snorkeling System

Putting on the Equipment

Exposure Suit

The exposure suit needs to be put on in the proper order at the proper time. Follow the steps in the right order. A general rule for dressing is to do it right before the dive. If you put on your wet suit too early you can become overheated.

Pants. From the hips down, fold the pants inside-out down to the knees. Slip the legs in up to your knees, then roll the pants up over your thighs and hips, making sure the crotch fits snugly.

2

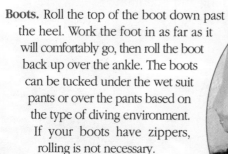

Boots. Roll the top of the boot down past the heel. Work the foot in as far as it will comfortably go, then roll the boot back up over the ankle. The boots can be tucked under the wet suit pants or over the pants based on the type of diving environment. If your boots have zippers, rolling is not necessary.

Hood. Holding the hood at the back, pull it from the forehead back over the top of the head so that your hair is completely covered. The skirt of the hood should be tucked neatly under the collar of the jacket. It may be easier to put the hood on first, then zip the jacket over it.

Jacket. Put the wet suit jacket on one arm at a time. Fit the sleeve openings around the wrists, then pull the sleeves all the way up to the underarms until they fit snugly without gaps or sags.

Gloves. The gloves are put on just like ordinary ones, but they must be pulled snugly onto the fingers and wrists. Many divers prefer to wait and put on the gloves later so the fingers are free for other equipment donning and adjustment. You may wish to leave only one hand ungloved, then put the other on after all adjustments are made. Overlap the sleeves of your wet suit with the gloves to cut down on water seepage.

Weight belt. When all the pieces of the suit are in place, put on the weight belt, if you are using one. Depending on the type of equipment you are using, you may need to put your weight belt on last. Your SSI Instructor will assist you when this is appropriate.

Snorkeling Vest/Buoyancy Compensator

The buoyancy compensator is easily donned when not yet combined with the cylinder for scuba use. Just put it on and make sure that it is snug, that the straps are properly adjusted and that it fits your body correctly.

If the vest is too loose it can ride up when you are swimming on the surface or entering the water. It must not interfere with the removal or ditching of the weight belt.

Mask

When putting on the mask, place it on your face and then pull the strap over the back of your head. The strap needs to be adjusted so that the mask is kept firmly and comfortably in place without over-tightening. When you have the strap where you want it, secure it.

Snorkel

The snorkel is positioned on the left side of the head (because the second-stage is positioned over the right shoulder) and is attached to the mask strap by a snorkel keeper. The snorkel should be positioned so that the mouthpiece is comfortable in the mouth, and the tube is straight up when the diver is looking down into the water.

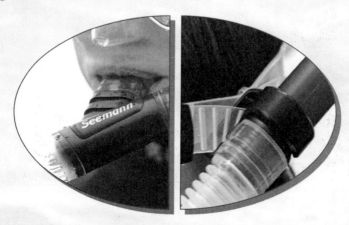

Fins

If you put them on while standing, secure yourself with one arm, then cross one leg over the other forming a figure "4" (think opposite hand, opposite foot) and pull on your fin. Because you become slightly less coordinated when wearing the fins on dry land, they are generally the last thing you put on and only when near your point of entry. Under some conditions, the fins can be donned after you enter the water.

The fins can be put on either from a sitting position or by standing and using a buddy for support.

When You Enter

After surfacing, clear the area before your buddy enters, then give the OK sign. Watch your buddy enter, being ready to assist if necessary. In fact, as a general rule always be aware of your buddy's condition and whereabouts.

Entering the Water

You should always use the best entry possible for the given circumstances. The best entry is the easiest and least disorienting one for the conditions. The entry should not jar or displace the equipment, and once you are in the water you should be able to see, breathe and float.

Before entering it is important to make a dive plan. Dive planning is covered in detail in subsequent chapters,

but here are a few important steps to take, as a buddy team, prior to the snorkel dive:

1. Decide where you will enter and which direction you will be going.

2. Decide where you will exit the water, making sure it's free of obstructions.

3. Find out if there are currents and which way they will carry you.

4. Complete a buddy check to make sure your equipment, as well as your buddy's, is assembled, adjusted and operating correctly.

5. Inflate your BC so that you will float after your entry.

6. Decide who will enter the water first or if you are on the beach, if you will enter together.

Beach Entry

If you enter on a beach with surf breaking near the shore, shuffle backwards with your fins on until deep enough to swim, then turn and swim out under or through the surf. If conditions are calm on shore, wade in without fins until about knee or waist deep, put them on there, then swim out. (Beach entries and exits will be covered in depth in Section 5.)

Sometimes you'll need to walk with your fins on, which can be awkward. It is easier and safer to shuffle backwards on pool and boat decks, on the shore and while entering and leaving shallow water.

The Controlled Seated Entry

The controlled seated entry is the easiest and least disorienting method to enter the water. It is done from low pool decks, docks or boat platforms, and only in calm water. While sitting on the edge with your legs dangling in the water. Follow these steps:

1. Place both hands on one side of your body, holding on to the platform if possible.

2. Support your body with your arms and turn and slip gently into the water.

The advantages of this entry are that you maintain stability by having constant contact with the platform, and that there is very little impact with the water.

The Step-in Entry

The step-in, or "giant stride," is the most common entry. It is done from a standing position on docks or boat dive-decks. The surface needs to be fairly firm so that balance can be maintained.

1. Position yourself with fins together at the edge of the entry point.

2. Hold the mask in place with one hand and the weight belt with the other.

3. Step out with one leg in front of the other — toes up, heels down — and enter the water with legs open "scissors" style. Step out far enough to completely clear the platform.

4. Hold your equipment in place until you surface and can see, breathe and float.

The Feet First Jumping Entry

A more appropriate entry from higher platforms is the feet first jumping entry. When you leave the entry platform, bring the fins together, and keep them positioned horizontally so that you land on the bottoms of your feet with your knees slightly bent to absorb the impact.

In the feet first jumping entry, the fins will slow your entry into the water considerably, but it will still be necessary to secure your mask and weight belt as you jump.

When using any method other than the seated entry, grip your mask and weight belt firmly to keep them in place during the entry, have the snorkel in your mouth and the BC inflated. Enter the water one at a time, making sure that the area of your entry is clear.

Using the Snorkel

Breathing with a snorkel is different from normal breathing. It is done in a three step process that helps ensure that you will always be able to breathe without interference from water in the tube.

1. Clear the snorkel by blowing a quick, sharp blast of air through it. This is called the popping method. You may need to clear again to remove any remaining water before breathing. Breathe cautiously through the snorkel.

2. Hold that breath so that you have another "blast" saved for clearing.

3. Get into the habit of this pattern: Clear, Breathe and Hold, then repeat.

Water will enter the snorkel when you dive under water. The way to clear the snorkel while under water and ascending to the surface is called the expansion method.

1. As you approach the surface, tilt your head back so that the snorkel tube is pointing downward.

2. Blow a small puff of air into it. This air expands due to lessening pressure as you rise toward the surface, and any remaining water is forced out. Note: Snorkels equipped with self-draining purge valves are cleared mostly by the force of gravity with each exhalation, but expansion may work with this kind of snorkel.

3. Any remaining water should be cleared by popping, just as with any other type of snorkel.

Using the Fins

Fins allow the diver to move through the water smoothly and with much less effort than without them.

The most common kick used with diving fins is a modified version of a swimmer's flutter kick.

1. The legs are kept elongated and the toes pointed.

2. The knees bend slightly and the relaxed ankles swing back and forth with the natural motion of the fins.

3. The stroke is slow and powerful, utilizing the full length of the legs; it is a "hip" kick, not a knee kick.

4. Keep your legs and fins under water when doing the flutter kick at the surface.

Fin Power

The power gained by using fins while swimming all but eliminates the need to use the hands or arms, which can be left relaxed at the sides, clasped in front of the body or carrying extra equipment. A comfortable diver will not use their hands, or arms for swimming, except when negotiating turns.

KNOWLEDGE · SKILLS
DIVER
DIAMOND
SSI
SCUBA SCHOOLS INTERNATIONAL
EQUIPMENT · EXPERIENCE

The power in the flutter kick comes from the leg making the downward stroke, while the leg making the upward stroke, or recovery stroke, is preparing for the next downward, power stroke. Thus, the power alternates from leg to leg with each kick.

The dolphin kick uses the whole body rather than just the legs. The legs are kept together and the body moves in a wavelike motion.

The dolphin kick has a graceful feel and is just for variety. It is also useful in case you lose a fin, or your calf becomes cramped under normal kicking circumstances. The dolphin kick works with just one or two fins. In fact, to practice the dolphin, take off one of your fins and lay one foot over the other.

One final note on fin kicks is to be aware whenever you are treading water in a vertical position over the reef. Your fins extend well past your feet and can cause damage to the reef by breaking coral structures, disturbing marine life or stirring up the bottom. Always look down to see where you are kicking.

Using the Snorkeling Vest

The joy of using a snorkel is that you can rest and relax face down on the surface and breathe at the same time. Wearing just a swimsuit or body suit with no added floatation, or weighted correctly with a wet suit and belt, most snorkelers will be able to rest and relax on the surface by simply floating face down, breathing through the snorkel. Some snorkelers may find that they feel more comfortable with a small amount of air in the vest, even while floating face down on the surface.

However, as snorkelers lift their heads up out of the water, they will need to kick or add buoyancy to support the weight of their heads out of the water. By inflating the vest, you can float effortlessly, head up, talk with your buddy, look around to stay oriented or enjoy the scenery above the water. Before you make a dive, if you have any air in your vest, deflate it by pushing the inflate/deflate button and squeezing the vest or by releasing the air at once if the vest is equipped with a dump valve. When you return to the surface, you have a choice of simply clearing your snorkel and returning to the face down position to rest or inflating your vest as needed. The easiest method for inflating a snorkeling vest or a diver's buoyancy compensator at the surface is called bobbing.

Inflate/Deflate Button

Emergency Inflation

If you ever need to inflate immediately in an emergency, some snorkeling vests are equipped with a CO$_2$ cartridge which inflates the vest at the pull of a cord. If you use a cartridge, be sure to replace it before using the vest again.

DIVER DIAMOND
SSI
KNOWLEDGE · SKILLS · EQUIPMENT · EXPERIENCE

To perform the bobbing technique:

1. Kick upward at the surface and inhale.

2. As you relax and sink back down into the water, exhale into the BC through the inflator hose.

3. Repeat the process. After a couple of repetitions the vest will be inflated enough to allow you to float.

Surface Dives

After becoming comfortable with your equipment at the surface, you will be ready to try some surface dives. There are two different surface dives: the "head-first dive" and the "feet-first dive." Both use the force of the body to push the diver down into the water, requiring very little energy. Before doing the dive you will need to release all the air from your BC.

To perform the head-first surface dive:

1. Start from a face down position with the body stretched out on the surface.

2. With a slight forward momentum, bend at the waist so that your upper body forms a right angle to your legs.

3. Lift the legs straight up and out of the water and reach toward the bottom.

Let the weight of your legs push you under water and begin your kick only after your fins have submerged.

When snorkeling, the feet-first dive is done primarily in kelp beds or where there is limited freedom of movement at the surface.

2

To perform the feet-first surface dive:

1.   Begin the dive in a floating, vertical position.

2.   Separate your legs, one forward and one back, and extend your arms away from your sides.

3.   Kick your legs together forcefully and sweep your arms down to the sides of your body at the same time. The objective is to lift the body above the surface swiftly, then drop smoothly under.

4.   When you are above water, keep your arms at your sides, your legs together and toes pointed down forming a "missile" to pierce the water and drop you well below the surface.

5.   Once under water, sweep your arms upward to force you further down, then tuck the body, roll forward and swim down.

As you ascend, look where you are going and extend an arm above your head to protect against obstructions. When you surface after a free dive, leave your mask on and snorkel in your mouth, move into the face down position and clear the snorkel. If you plan on staying on the surface for a while, inflate your BC. If you plan to dive again soon, you can remain buoyant at the surface by keeping your lungs fairly full between breaths and remaining face down.

One up, One Down

When snorkeling with your buddy , it's a good safety plan to follow the one up, one down system. While one of you dives, the other stays on the surface. The diver on the surface can watch the diver below, and be ready to assist if that diver should encounter trouble of any kind.

While You Descend — Equalizing Pressure

Equalizing Mask Pressure

Unless pressure inside the mask is increased so that it equals increasing outside pressure, the suction created can cause an injury called a mask squeeze.

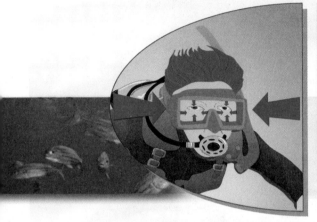

Exhale gently through your nose to equalize the pressure inside your mask.

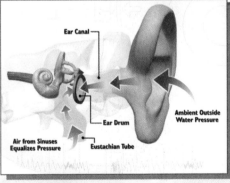

Equalizing Ear Pressure

Ear squeezes are avoided by pinching the nose closed with thumb and index finger, then attempting to gently exhale through the nose. This equalizes the middle ear against the force of the water pressing in from the outside. Yawning, swallowing, wiggling the jaw can also be used to help equalize the ears while diving.

If you have a problem equalizing as you descend, stop, or ascend a few feet until you are successful and the discomfort subsides. Never disregard pain or discomfort. If equalization is not possible, do not dive.

2

Equalizing Sinus Pressure

Sinus cavities will normally equalize themselves as you descend. If sinus openings are blocked by congestion from colds, allergies, infection or some other sinus condition, you may experience a painful sinus squeeze. You cannot dive unless your sinuses can equalize. Divers with chronic sinus ailments should seek the counsel of a dive medicine physician before diving.

Equalizing

Be careful not to blow too hard while your nose and mouth are shut — this can cause injury to the inner ear. Also, be sure to release your nose each time after you equalize so that you can exhale into your mask to avoid mask squeeze.

To avoid problems with equalizing, begin before you descend, as you submerge, and continually as you descend. Never wait for discomfort to occur, but equalize before discomfort has a chance to occur.

Exits

Always exit the best and easiest way possible for conditions. If you are using a ladder to exit onto a pool, boat deck, or a raised platform such as a dock you will need to either remove your fins and lay them on the deck or hook an arm through the fin straps, if equipped, and climb up.

Never climb a ladder wearing fins unless the ladder is designed for this use.

If you are going to remove equipment and hand it up to boat or dock personnel, leave your fins on until you are ready to actually exit.

Your SSI Dealer offers a variety of Specialty Courses, including Boat Diving, that include techniques regarding entering and exiting the water in different circumstances.

If you are making a shore exit, swim or crawl to a place where you can easily stand up and remove your fins, then walk up. Shore exits will be covered in depth in Section 5.

Whenever making an exit, keep enough air in your BC to float in case you fall back into the water.

Scuba Diving

Assembling the Scuba Unit

There is a standard sequence for assembly of the scuba unit. Do it the same way every time to ensure that nothing is ever left out.

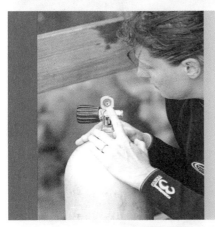

1. **Examine the cylinder and valve for overall condition.** Open valve gently to clear any possible debris from the opening and then do a quick air sniff. (If there is any odor, do not use that cylinder. Scuba air should be clean, dry, and odorless.) Inspect the O-ring after you close the valve. Replace it if it is missing, cut or badly abraded. Turn the cylinder so that the valve opening points away from you.

2. **Attach Buoyancy Compensator to Cylinder.** Start with the cylinder retaining band buckling mechanism facing you. This puts the cylinder between you and the BC. Check buckling mechanism for condition. Slide the band over the cylinder (your instructor will show you the exact location to place the band as it may vary depending on the type of BC you are using). The band should lock solidly and show no stress cracks or distortion. Lift the unit by holding the BC straps in one hand and the cylinder retaining band in the other. The cylinder should not slip. If it does, the retaining assembly needs to be tightened.

1. You may need to wet the retaining band, as nylon tends to stretch when wet.

2. Be sure to check the BC service tag to ensure that the BC has been serviced properly.

3. **Check the Regulator.** Remove the dust cover from the first-stage yoke and check the filter. It should be grey in color, with no debris present. If it is any color other than grey, or if there is any debris attached to the filter, have the regulator checked by your SSI Dealer prior to using it to dive. Check the second-stage mouthpiece for any foreign objects.

4. **Attach the Regulator to the Cylinder.** With the first-stage in your left hand and the second-stage in your right, so that the second-stage is routed over the right shoulder of the BC, drop the regulator yoke over the cylinder valve. Align the first-stage yoke or DIN orifice so that it mates into the cylinder valve opening, then lightly hand tighten to the yoke or screw (DIN connection) until firmly seated.

Because of the high pressure and o-ring seal, tightening the yoke or DIN by hand is all that is necessary to establish a properly tensioned connection.

5. **Attach Low-pressure Inflator.** Attach the low-pressure hose to the BC low-pressure inflator hose.

Before you turn on the air:

◆ Attempt to exhale through each second-stage. Unlike inhaling, you should be able to exhale easily. If you can not, the exhaust valve may be stuck shut. You can usually remedy this by immersing the regulator in water to dilute the light adhesive force that has formed between the exhaust valve and the second-stage housing and then attempting to exhale through the second-stage again. Once the valve begins to allow easy exhalation, make sure you still can not inhale. This will ensure that the exhaust valve is functioning properly.

◆ Gently attempt to inhale from each second-stage. If you can inhale, there is a problem with the integrity of the second-stage. Either the diaphragm has a hole or the exhaust valves are dislodged or missing. Do not use the regulator until it has been checked and cleared by your SSI Dealer.

◆ Check the mouthpieces for condition and proper attachment. The mouthpiece should be whole with no surface cracks evident. Mouthpieces are attached to second-stages with tie wraps. The tie wraps should be in position, tight and should easily hold the mouthpiece in place even if tugged on.

◆ Check the gauges. Both pressure gauge and depth gauge should register zero at this point.

◆ Turn gauge face down and away from yourself and others.

6. **Slowly pressurize the system.** If you hear a leak, stop and determine the problem. No leaks. Open valve all the way. Check the submersible pressure gauge to make sure cylinder has adequate air. Perform the inhale/exhale test again, this time observing pressure gauge.

Any fluctuation in the needle indicates an obstruction or a partially closed valve. First check to ensure that the cylinder valve is open. If the valve is not the problem, have your regulator checked or serviced by your SSI Dealer.

7. Inflate and deflate BC. Inflate and deflate the BC both orally and with the power inflator to determine proper function of inflator and exhaust valves.

2

8. Lay down the scuba unit. Once the scuba unit is assembled, lay it down on its side in an easily accessible place or secure it in a special rack designed to hold it upright.

Putting on the Scuba Unit

There are three basic methods for getting into your scuba unit:

1. **From a sitting position.** The sitting position is the most convenient but cannot be used in all situations. Dive boats are usually equipped with a scuba unit station or platform upon which the diver sets the scuba unit until it is time to dive.

2. **From a standing position with help from your buddy.** While standing with your back to your buddy, have him or her lift the scuba unit high enough for you to slip your arms into the BC, then hold it there while you make adjustments. The buddy should hold the cylinder at top and bottom.

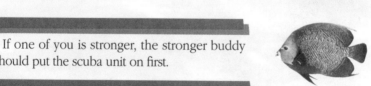

If one of you is stronger, the stronger buddy should put the scuba unit on first.

3. **In the water.** The method for putting on the scuba unit while in the water will vary according to circumstances. Some dive boats will be equipped with a float line on which the unit will be sent out to the diver. The diver's buddy would then assist in putting it on and adjusting it. There are also methods for donning the scuba unit in the water without help.

Be Aware

Regardless of your method of putting on the unit, make sure the BC does not interfere with the weight belt, which must be free and positioned for easy ditching. If your BC is weight integrated, make sure your weight pockets are there and you fully understand how to ditch the weights in the event of an emergency.

The Pre-Entry Buddy Check

The pre-entry buddy check is a precautionary procedure where you and your buddy will check each other's equipment, assist with adjustments and generally make sure you are both ready for entry into the water.

◆ Do a visual inspection of your buddy from top to bottom. Is the mask strap in place? Are hoses and gauges routed correctly and kept neatly in place so they will not snag or drag? Is the BC buckled and snug? Is the weight release system accessible? You do not want any equipment left loose or dangling. Loose equipment is susceptible to damage, is difficult to locate under water and can damage valuable marine life.

◆ Do a hands-on inspection. Check to see if your buddy's cylinder valve is open, then look at the pressure gauge to make sure the cylinder has a sufficient supply of air. Check to see where your buddy's alternate air source is located and that it is properly secured. Also make sure you know how to operate your buddy's weight system.

Your primary concern in doing the pre-entry buddy check is that you are both ready to enter the water. If for any reason you or your buddy are not completely confident that "all systems are go," do not enter the water until you are.

Controlled Seated

Scuba Entries

Entry methods for both scuba and snorkeling are identical. However, more complications can arise in entering with full scuba equipment because of extra weight and bulk. Make your entry knowing you and your equipment will be clear of any obstacles, including the platform from which you are entering, or with anything in the water.

You may go under water when entering, so always keep your mask on so you can see, the regulator in your mouth so you can breathe and the BC inflated so you can float.

Step-in

Jump In

Using the Mask

Warm air inside the lens condenses when cool water surrounds the mask. This causes the lens to fog and restrict vision. Eliminate this problem by cleaning your mask thoroughly with a commercial mask cleaner and coating the inside of the lens with a commercial anti-fogging solution before getting the mask wet.

By now you have encountered the term "clearing the mask" a few times. In snorkeling, this is a simple procedure. Small amounts of water will inevitably get into the mask. To clear your mask come to the surface, or stand up if necessary, and lift the bottom of the mask with your thumbs, letting the water run out.

Mask Cleaning

If you are using a new mask, you must first clean off a silicone film, which coats the inside of the lens before using anti-fog. Do this with a commercial mask cleaning agent and water.

KNOWLEDGE SKILLS
DIVER DIAMOND
SSI
EQUIPMENT EXPERIENCE

To clear your mask under water:

1. Gently push the top part of the mask against the forehead while looking slightly up.

2. Exhale steadily and slowly through the nose while tipping your head back so that you are looking upward. Your exhaled air will displace the water and move it easily out the bottom of the mask. If your mask is equipped with a purge valve,

position the water at the lowest part of the mask, hold the mask snugly against your face and exhale slowly through your nose.

Using the Second-Stage Regulator

Breathing with the second-stage is easy once you become familiar with it. The method for breathing through the second-stage is a slow, steady inhalation followed by a relaxed exhalation. Do not rush. Relax and let the air flow out naturally each time you exhale.

It is important to develop the habit of breathing all the time through the second-stage. Never hold your breath. If the second-stage is out of your mouth, teach yourself to exhale a continuous, steady stream of bubbles. Always remember to breathe and keep your breathing rhythm slow and deep.

Clearing the Second-Stage

Any time water enters the regulator mouthpiece, you'll need to clear it. The most common way to clear it is to exhale with slightly more force than usual into the mouthpiece, expelling water through the exhaust valve. The second-stage can also be cleared by lightly pressing the second-stage purge button for a moment. Always inhale cautiously after clearing.

Retrieving the Second-Stage

If the second-stage comes out of your mouth while under water, remember first to keep exhaling and not to hold your breath. To retrieve the second-stage:

Second-Stage Purge Button

2

1. Swing your right arm down and to your side and hook the second-stage hose from underneath.

2. If you are not able to locate it immediately, rotate or lean your body slightly to the right so that gravity pulls the second-stage down into view (your buddy can also help).

3. When you have the regulator in hand and you are ready to replace it, you will need to clear it before inhaling again.

4. After clearing, inhale slowly, making sure there is no water left inside the mouthpiece.

Another method is to reach over your shoulder for the first-stage yoke attached at the cylinder valve and follow the hose down to the second-stage with your hand. When you have got the second-stage regulator in your hand, continue with steps 3 and 4 listed above.

If you cannot locate your primary second-stage, another option is to breathe off your alternate air source until your primary can be located.

Snorkel Use in Scuba Diving

The snorkel is used for certain reasons while scuba diving:

♦ Preserving cylinder air while moving around at the surface,

♦ Surface swimming from entry points to points of descent, and from points of ascent to exit points, and

♦ In surging or choppy water conditions where there is a possibility of inhaling water, such as when exiting on shore with surf, some divers may choose to use the air delivery system.

DIVER DIAMOND
KNOWLEDGE · SKILLS · EQUIPMENT · EXPERIENCE
SSI SCUBA SCHOOLS INTERNATIONAL

Surface Procedures

On the surface, always keep enough air in your BC so that you can comfortably float without kicking and make any necessary adjustments.

Descending

The scuba descent needs to be done slowly and started from an upright position so the diver can control the rate of descent to equalize gradually, avoid impact with the bottom and avoid going beyond prescribed depth limits.

1. To start your descent, begin in a feet-first position.

2. Hold the inflator hose above your head in your left hand and let air escape the BC by depressing the deflate button or pulling down on the inflator mechanism to operate the dump valve.

3. Once the BC is completely deflated, exhale and relax to get yourself under the water. You may need to do a feet-first surface dive to get yourself started through the first few feet.

Never help your buddy by pulling him or her under water on descent unless you have been asked to help. Assisting a buddy when he or she is not expecting it can lead to problems!

4. As the buoyancy of the wet suit decreases due to compression, add small amounts of air to the BC to help control your descent.

5. As you approach the depth at which you would like to stabilize, add more air to the BC, if needed, to become suspended in the water. Your objective is to establish neutral buoyancy, a condition of neither sinking nor floating up.

♦ Be careful not to add too much air because this will make you positively buoyant and cause you to begin ascending. Adding short bursts of air is best.

6. Look down periodically as you descend to watch where you are going. This will help you avoid collision with a coral reef or any marine life.

Using the BC

In scuba diving the BC is used in four basic ways:

1. Floating at the surface,

2. Controlling descents,

3. Establishing and maintaining neutral buoyancy at depth, and

4. Aiding in ascents.

KNOWLEDGE *SKILLS* *DIVER DIAMOND* *SSI* *EQUIPMENT* *EXPERIENCE*

Neutral Buoyancy During Your Dive

As you change depths during your dive, you will learn to adjust your buoyancy to enjoy the pleasure and freedom of remaining neutral in the water. When you go deeper, adding air to your BC will keep you from sinking. When you move into shallower water, releasing air will keep you from floating up. An easy check for neutral buoyancy is to stop all movement, inhale fully and see if you float up a little. Then, exhale fully and you should feel yourself sink.

Buoyancy

A diver suspended in mid-water with buoyancy equalized will float gently up and down with each breathing cycle. Improving your buoyancy skills is fun to practice and helps make your diving easier and more comfortable.

KNOWLEDGE *SKILLS* *DIVER DIAMOND* *SSI* *EQUIPMENT* *EXPERIENCE*

Ascending and Surfacing

You and your buddy should decide when you want to ascend, signal each other that you are ready, and then ascend together. Your goal is a slow, effortless ascent with a safety stop at 15 feet (4.5 metres).

1. Become neutrally buoyant before starting your ascent. If you are not, add a small amount of air to your BC to achieve neutral buoyancy.

2. Use a gentle fin kick to begin ascending upward.

As you ascend, pressure will decrease, and this will cause your BC to become more positively buoyant. This will help you to ascend and will allow you to kick without effort.

Dive Lines

It is a good idea to use a line for both descents and ascents if the environmental conditions and dive site allow for it. Lines allow you to stay with your buddy, better control your rate of ascent and descent, and stop to equalize pressure or handle minor emergencies. During your training the Instructor will make the decision whether a line is appropriate. Upon certification, you should consider the value of using a line each time you dive.

3. Use your computer or depth gauge and timer to manage your rate of ascent. Most computers have an ascent rate indicator that will flash or show a message when you are ascending too fast.

◆ The air inside your BC will expand as you ascend and make you increasingly buoyant.

◆ Depress the deflate button or pull the dump cord and allow some air to escape as you go up.

◆ Keep an eye on your computer or depth gauge and timing device, making sure you do not exceed 30 feet (9 metres) per minute. If you are using a depth gauge and timer to monitor your ascent rate, 30 feet (9 metres) should take 60 seconds to complete.

Do Not Exceed 30 Feet (9 Metres) Per Minute

◆ As you approach 15 feet (4.5 metres), release enough air from your BC to stop your ascent and hover neutral, at 15 feet (4.5 metres) for a safety stop. Safety stops will be explained in more detail in Section 4.

4. Look up and listen for boats while you ascend, making sure your path is clear.

15' (4.5 metres)

Make sure to breathe normally at all times, and pay special attention to breathing normally as you ascend — the lungs can be damaged on ascent if you hold your breath. This is explained in more detail in Section 3.

5. Again, on any ascent, do not try and assist your buddy unless you have been asked to help. Assisting your buddy when it is not expected can lead to problems.

6. When you surface, leave your mask on and your regulator in your mouth, and inflate your BC.

7. After stabilizing, you can change to snorkel breathing to save cylinder air.

Exits

As with entries, your primary concern in exiting the water is doing it the best and easiest way possible. Variations on exiting are based on environmental factors and the type of diving you are doing. As a general rule, when exiting, leave your equipment in place and your BC inflated until you are safely out of the water. Be sure to have an exit point and exit method planned even before entering the water.

Boat Exits

If you are exiting the water onto a boat, the method will depend mostly on the boat captain or dive leader's preference. They may advise you either to remove your fins and climb up or remove equipment while in the water and hand it up first. If you are removing equipment in the water, start with the weight belt.

Though some methods will differ, here are a few general rules to follow:

1. Never climb a ladder with fins on, unless the ladder is designed for this use.

2. Make sure there is air in your BC when you take it off in water.

3. Always assist your buddy in maintaining stability and removing and handing up equipment.

2

Shore Exits

When making an exit in calm water conditions and on a shore with a gradual incline, such as a sandy beach, you and your buddy should swim together to a place where you can safely help each other remove your fins, then stand and walk up onto the beach.

In surf or in an area where there is some sort of abrupt approach to the beach, such as a ledge, allow the water to bring you shoreward as far as possible, then crawl to a point at which it is safe to remove fins and walk up.

Summary

So far, we have discussed what the subsystems of the Total Diving System are and how they work. You have learned why a diver needs each piece of equipment and how to use it. Now, you understand why high quality equipment is an integral part of the Diver Diamond and how it contributes to your comfort as a diver.

In the next sections, we will build upon your newly acquired equipment knowledge by discussing how diving and pressure affects you and your equipment and how to plan a safe dive.

Section 2 Study Guide Questions

1. The exposure suit needs to be put on in the proper order at the proper time. Follow the steps in the right order. A general rule for dressing is to do it _____ _____ the _____.

2. Depending on the type of equipment you are using, you may need to put the _____ _____ on last.

3. Sometimes you'll need to walk with your fins on, which can be awkward. It is easier and safer to shuffle backwards on _____ and _____ decks, on the _____, and while entering and leaving _____ water.

4. The most common kick used with diving fins is a modified version of the swimmer's _____ kick.

5. The power gained by using fins while swimming all but eliminates the need to use the _____ or _____, which can be left relaxed at the sides, clasped in front of the body or carrying extra equipment.

6. Your fins extend well past your feet and can cause _____ to the reef by breaking coral structures, disturbing marine life or stirring up the bottom. Always look down down to see where you are _____.

7. As you _____, look where you are going and extend one _____ above your head to protect against obstructions.

8. When snorkeling with your buddy, it's a good safety plan to follow the _____ _____, _____ _____ system.

9. _____ gently through your _____ to equalize the pressure inside your mask.

10. Ear squeezes are avoided by _____ the nose closed with the _____ and index finger, then attempting to _____ exhale through the nose.

11. Scuba Unit Assembly.
    1) Inflate and deflate the BC.
    2) Slowly pressurize the system.
    3) Attach the Regulator to the Cylinder.
    4) Lay Down the Scuba Unit.
    5) Check the Regulator.
    6) Attach Buoyancy Compensator to the cylinder.
    7) Attach the Low-pressure Inflator.
    Circle the correct order in which the Scuba Unit should be assembled.
    a) 2, 3, 5, 6, 7, 1, 4
    b) 6, 5, 3, 7, 2, 1, 4
    c) 6, 5, 7, 3, 1 ,2 ,4
    d) 5, 6, 2, 1, 7, 3, 4
    e) 4, 1, 2, 7, 3, 6, 5

12. Regardless of your method of putting on the unit, make sure the _____ does not interfere with the weight belt, which must be free and positioned for easy ditching.

13. If for any reason you or your buddy are not completely confident that _____ _____ _____ _____, don't enter the water until you are.

14. You may go under water when entering, so always keep your _____ on so you can see, the _____ in your mouth so you can breathe, and the _____ inflated so you can float.

15. The method for breathing through the second stage is a slow, steady _____ followed by a relaxed _____.

16. If you cannot locate your primary second-stage, another option is to breathe off your _____ _____ _____ until your primary can be located.

17. As you approach the depth at which you would like to stabilize, add more air to the _____, if needed, to become _____ in the water.

18. You and your buddy should decide when you want to ascend, signal each other that you are ready, then ascend together. Your goal is a _____, effortless ascent with a _____ _____ at 15 feet (4.5 metres).

19. Keep an eye on your _____ or _____ _____ and timing device, making sure you do not exceed 30 feet (9 metres) per minute. If you are using a depth gauge and timer to monitor your ascent rate, 30 feet (9 metres) should take _____ seconds to complete.

20. As a general rule, when exiting leave your _____ in place and your BC _____ until you are safely out of the water.

SCUBA SCHOOLS
INTERNATIONAL

Your Body and the Underwater World

SECTION 3

3

"As knowledge increases,
wonder deepens."

— Charles Morgan

Have you ever wondered what the lure of diving is? What possesses someone to look forward for months to a diving vacation in the Caribbean, or even to devote his or her life to underwater exploration? Well, just imagine an inner city teenager from New York donning a backpack and ascending to the summit of a 14,000 foot (or 4.2 kilometre) peak in the Rocky Mountains for the first time. A new environment can be a thrill—sometimes enough of a thrill to make you want to stay or, at least, visit often.

For the scuba diver that new environment is always nearby, and the experience can be prolonged, repeated and made a part of your life. What makes diving accessible is that water is always with us and is everywhere we go; what makes it possible is that the human body can be adapted to function in water almost as well as it does on dry land.

Section 3 Objectives
After completing this section you will

◆ Understand the effects of increasing pressure on your body and, the Total Diving System,

◆ Understand how breathing compressed gas affects your body,

◆ Understand the basic functions of respiration,

◆ Understand partial pressures and how they apply to you as a diver,

◆ Know basic procedures to adapt to the underwater environment,

◆ Know proper ascent procedures under normal and emerging conditions and

◆ Know the causes, treatment and prevention of Nitrogen Narcosis, Decompression Sickness and overexpansion injuries.

Effects of Increasing Pressure

Right now we are not aware of the air pressure surrounding our bodies at sea level because it is evenly applied in all directions. When ascending to a higher altitude, you may experience your ears "popping". This represents a mild pressure change.

Pressure

Pressure is defined as a force per unit area and is commonly expressed in pounds per square inch (PSI), bar and atmospheres (ATM).

We have all experienced the effects of increasing pressure when swimming. Many of us remember what it was like as a youngster to dive for coins at our local swimming pool or to go down and touch the drain. There was always that discomfort in those last few feet when the pressure began to make our ears hurt. The reason for our discomfort was that pressure increases very fast as you descend.

As a diver you need to know how changes in pressure affect your body and how to compensate for them.

Ambient Pressure

Ambient pressure, or "surrounding pressure," as applied to diving, refers to the sum of air pressure and water pressure.

The reason a diver experiences discomfort or pain in the ears at a depth as shallow as ten feet, as in the case of the youngster diving for coins, is that water is much more dense, and therefore heavier than air, and its pressure increases rapidly as you go deeper.

Atmospheric Pressure

At sea level, atmospheric pressure is about 14.7 psi (1 bar). That is the measure of the downward force of air in an imaginary one-inch (25 mm) square column from the top of the atmosphere to sea level, about 60 miles (96 km).

Equalizing Pressure

The human body is made up of approximately 70% by volume of liquids and about 30% solids and gases. Liquids and solids are not compressible.

KNOWLEDGE SKILLS
DIVER DIAMOND
SSI
EQUIPMENT EXPERIENCE

Boyle's Law

Depth Feet/Metres	ATM	Ambient Pressure PSI/bar	Volume of a Sealed Container	Density of Gas
0/0	1	14.7/1	1	1x
33/10	2	29.4/2	1/2	2x
66/20	3	44.1/3	1/3	3x
99/30	4	58.8/4	1/4	4x

Humans have areas of the body which contain gases. Included in this part of our makeup are air spaces—the sinuses, middle ears, and lungs.

Unlike water and solids, gases are compressible. At 33 feet (10 metres), where the body is under two atmospheres of pressure (without equalization), the volume of the body's flexible air spaces would be reduced by one half. As described in Section 1, this is due to Boyle's Law.

**0 feet/
0 metres**

**33 feet/
10 metres**

**66 feet/
20 metres**

Air Space

There are air spaces within the diver's body and equipment which are subject to squeezes, and for each there is a method of equalizing.

DIVER
DIAMOND
SSI

KNOWLEDGE · SKILLS · EQUIPMENT · EXPERIENCE

3

To keep the shape of the body's air spaces the same as on the surface, as the diver descends (into increasing pressure), air needs to be added until the pressure inside of the air spaces is equal to the pressure outside of the air spaces. This is called equalizing the pressure.

Without equalization the diver will experience a squeeze.

Ears Under Water

The eardrum acts as a wall between water and air. An ear squeeze occurs when water pressure in the ear canal pushes harder against the outside of the ear-drum than the air pressure pushing from the inside.

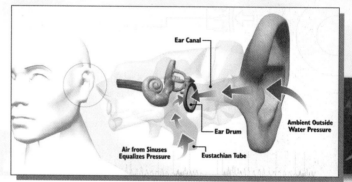

Ear Canal

Air from Sinuses Equalizes Pressure

Ear Drum

Eustachian Tube

Ambient Outside Water Pressure

To equalize ears, pinch the nose shut and blow gently into the nose. This will allow air pressure to pass from the lungs through the eustachian tubes into the middle ear. Sometimes it is easier to equalize ears by wiggling the jaw, swallowing, or yawning.

◆ Ear equalization, or "clearing," should be started immediately upon descending and continued as you dive deeper, and it should never be done forcefully. In fact, you can test for equalization at the surface by gently clearing.

♦ Failure to equalize the ears can result in injury. Rupture of the eardrum can result from unequalized ears, even in very shallow water. Damage can also occur when a diver tries to equalize too forcefully when the ears are blocked.

♦ The greatest percentage of pressure change is close to the surface, especially in the 15-20 foot (4.5-6 metre) range.

♦ If at any point in your descent you have difficulty equalizing your ears, stop your descent, go up a few feet to lessen the pressure and slowly try your descent again.

♦ Symptoms of an ear injury can include ear pain, dizziness, nausea, and difficulty hearing. Victims of ear injury should seek medical attention.

Sinuses

The passageways into your sinus cavities are normally open. So, when you take a breath from your second-stage, air flows from your mouth into your sinuses and equalizes the pressure. Sinus cavities will equalize themselves as long as the passageways are open.

♦ Sinus equalization can be hampered by a blockage of the opening to the sinuses created by swelling or congestion due to colds, allergies, infection or some other disorder. This can result in pain in the forehead, between the eyes, in the cheekbones and sometimes in the upper teeth.

Hoods

Hoods can trap air in the ear canal which may cause difficulty in equalizing the pressure in the ears. To help prevent this, you can pull the hood away from the head to let water into the hood. This lets in water so that the pressure can be equalized. If possible, exhaling air into the hood can also help.

KNOWLEDGE **SKILLS**
DIVER DIAMOND **SSI** SCUBA SCHOOLS INTERNATIONAL
EQUIPMENT **EXPERIENCE**

♦ If your sinuses are blocked, it is best not to dive until the problem is resolved and they are open again.

Equipment

A squeeze will be felt most commonly in the mask. The space it encloses is large compared to the middle ear and sinuses, and unless that space is equalized you will feel the mask tighten against your face and eyes.

To equalize the mask, gently exhale through the nose into the mask until it feels comfortable again.

Lungs

As a swimmer or a snorkeler, when you take a breath, hold it and descend; the air in your lungs compresses and the volume of your lungs decreases, just as if you were exhaling. This is not dangerous because you would have to swim down to an extreme depth for this compression to become a problem.

When scuba diving, every time you take a breath from your second-stage it delivers air at the same pressure as the surrounding water (ambient pressure).

Breathing Underwater

Breathing is not something we usually pay attention to. But under water you become acutely aware of breathing. Your mind and body know you are out of your element and are telling you so. While you can overcome the unfamiliar environment with equipment, you will require knowledge and training to compensate for various physiological differences. You need to know that while gases are exchanged in underwater breathing just as they are on land, pressure changes affect the amounts of those gases and the rates of their exchange.

Diving Fitness

Statistics show that diving is not a hazardous activity. When accidents do occur, they often involve divers who are in some way predisposed to risk. Certain risk factors are environmental, but many are individual.

A healthy individual simply makes a better diver. There are certain practices and precautions that will make the difference in recreational diving being tiring and uncomfortable or effortless and exciting. Some of these have to do more with short term diving preparation, such as getting plenty of sleep and not consuming alcohol the night before a dive. Others are more long term, such as maintaining a good diet, participating in a regular exercise program and getting regular medical checkups, especially if you

♦ Smoke,

♦ Have had recent surgery,

♦ Are over 45,

♦ Are overweight,

♦ Are on medication (consult your physician) and/or

♦ Have heart, respiratory or other medical problems that might warrant concern.

Cardiovascular Fitness

Some think diving is relatively nonphysical. Although the activity of diving is not high tempo, it is done in the heavy medium of water. Diving requires strength, and is done for extensive periods, which requires stamina. For diving, it is recommended you get a medical checkup. After determining that you are in good health, do a little "tuning up" by exercising your heart and lungs. Common aerobic exercises include jogging, cycling, swimming, aerobic dance and sports in which cardiovascular activity is sustained.

Cardiovascular fitness also provides increased circulation. This helps keep divers warmer longer, helps them stay alert, which is important in problem solving, and also requires less work for the lungs in getting oxygen into the blood, which allows the diver to consume less air.

Healthy Lungs

Efficient lungs are very important to reduce risk in diving. Even very healthy divers can have difficulty because of lung problems, either temporary or chronic. Aerobic fitness can help in that it guards against carbon dioxide buildup. But sometimes fitness is not enough.

Anything that restricts the flow of air in and out of the lungs or the exchange of gases in the respiratory system can make certain divers more susceptible to problems. For this reason, divers who have colds or flu, have chronic sinus ailments, which cause excessive phlegm or blockage of the sinuses or bronchial tubes, or have asthma should seek the counsel of a dive physician.

> ### Using Medication
>
> It is recommended that you either dive only when you are well or after getting the consent of your physician to use medication while diving.

It is possible to dive while using a medication that helps eliminate the symptoms of an illness or disorder, but it is important to be aware of possible side effects, such as drowsiness, which in turn may impair judgement. It is also not known at this time what, if any, effects pressure and depth have on the human body while on medication. Of course, a precaution everyone can take to ensure better lung health is not to smoke.

Breath Control: Stress Control

Given healthy lungs, other breathing problems can be related to anxiety or fear under water. A common reaction to anxiety or fear is a rapid, shallow breathing pattern. Shallow breathing can then lead to an out-of-breath feeling. The way to manage anxiety and stress and avoid panic is simple. Slow your breathing down by focusing on the exhale in order to return to normal breathing, which (as described in Section 2) is a slow, steady inhalation followed by a relaxed exhale, which lets the air flow out naturally. This may not be the way you breathe all the time above or under water, but it is what we mean when we say "breathe normally" under water.

The physical tension created by fear makes a relaxed exhalation difficult. By focusing on the exhalation, relaxing and letting the air flow out, you actually calm yourself down and return to normal breathing. This also helps calm your body by slowing the breathing rate and lowering carbon dioxide levels. Managing your breathing is your most important diving stress management technique.

Follow these easy procedures to control anxiety and stress when a difficulty arises:

1. **Stop what you are doing.**

2. **Focus on returning to "normal breathing" until you are relaxed and in control.**

3. **Think about what to do next.**

A "difficulty" may be something as simple as an ill-fitting wet suit which restricts movement, gradually making you breathe harder because of extra physical exertion. By consciously returning your breathing to normal and remaining calm and alert, you can avert stress and allow yourself to respond logically. This is not hard to do. Remember that you are there to enjoy your dive. If anything interferes with that, take care of it immediately but calmly, and keep breathing normally.

The Functioning of the Lungs

Speaking of the lungs as something isolated inside the body, as we usually do, is not really correct. The lungs are part of a complex system that circulates throughout the body, bringing fuel to the cells and eliminating waste.

The lungs themselves are made up of clusters of elastic sacs and are suspended from air tubes. The windpipe connects the throat and the lungs. This pipe splits off in a "Y", sending air into the two separate lungs; the air is brought into the lungs by smaller airways called the bronchial tubes. These lead through smaller and smaller airways to clusters of tiny sacs at the inside of the lung membrane called alveoli. Each tiny sac, or alveolus, is constructed of blood capillaries and membrane. This is where the transfer of gases in and out of the blood takes place.

Gas Exchange

The physical process of the lungs correlates with a biological process. When you inhale, the alveoli fill with air, and oxygen is then absorbed into the bloodstream through the network of capillaries,

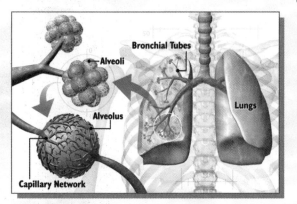

Bronchial Tubes

Alveoli

Alveolus

Lungs

Capillary Network

which help to form the outer membrane of each alveolus.

As the blood circulates through the body, the cells are fed this oxygen. The cells then give off the waste product carbon dioxide.

Carbon dioxide has a very important role in this continuous process: Carbon dioxide again builds up and this signals the body to inhale again, and so on.

Another gas that plays a role in this process is nitrogen. Although oxygen is the gas which sustains life, it only constitutes about 20% of the air you breathe, while about 80% is nitrogen.

Nitrogen is actually an inert gas and is not used by the body.

CO_2

Carbon dioxide tells the body when to breathe. It is a buildup of carbon dioxide rather than a lack of oxygen that stimulates the respiratory center of the brain to direct the diaphragm muscle to pull down and the rib cage to widen. The expanded area in the lungs drops the pressure and air flows in to equalize. When the diaphragm and rib cage relax, air is squeezed out by the elasticity in the air sacs.

Overexertion and excitement can cause you to breathe very fast and shallow. This shallow breathing can then lead to an adverse chain reaction:

♦ Shallow breathing does not allow carbon dioxide to be vented off fully,

♦ This retained carbon dioxide buildup then signals the need to breathe sooner than normal,

♦ Short, quick breaths can then prevent the exchange of a large enough amount of air in the lungs,

♦ This causes the person to breathe harder to try to compensate for feeling out of breath,

♦ Which in turn causes anxiety, further complicating things.

> ### Prevention
> Where your comfort and enjoyment is concerned, prevention is the best answer.

Unless a diver stops, thinks and gets breathing under control, stress, and even panic, may result.

Sustained shallow breathing and/or overexertion can cause an excess of carbon dioxide in the diver's body. Symptoms include:

♦ Labored breathing

♦ Shortness of breath

♦ Headache

To prevent carbon dioxide excess, avoid overexertion and dive with high quality, well-maintained equipment.

Any time breathlessness occurs, stop and rest until breathing is normal. The symptoms will disappear when the cause is eliminated.

Develop a pattern of inhaling steadily and slowly, followed by a relaxed, steady exhalation. Inhalation and exhalation should be done one after the other without pause.

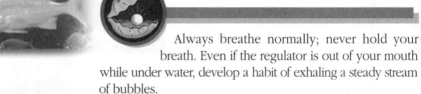

Always breathe normally; never hold your breath. Even if the regulator is out of your mouth while under water, develop a habit of exhaling a steady stream of bubbles.

Effects of Breathing Compressed Air: Partial Pressures

Breathing at the Surface

Air is a mixture of gases, about 20% oxygen and 80% nitrogen. At sea level we breathe air at 14.7 psi or 1 bar of pressure. Since 20% of the total is oxygen, the pressure of oxygen in air at sea level is 2.94 psi or .2 bar (20% of 14.7 psi/1 bar). The pressure of nitrogen at sea level is then 11.76 psi (.8 bar) (80% of 14.7 psi/1 bar). This is expressed in a simple law of physics called Dalton's Law, which explains that the pressure of a gas mixture is made up of the sum of the partial pressures of the gases in that mixture.

After we take oxygen and nitrogen into the lungs, the gases move through our bodies serving different purposes—the oxygen is our body's fuel and is required to sustain life.

♦ The blood in our circulatory system picks up the oxygen and carries it to our tissues.

♦ At the tissue level, the oxygen is used and in the process produces carbon dioxide, which is then carried by the blood back to the lungs and exhaled.

Nitrogen is not needed by the body and is not used or processed, but just like oxygen, it is a gas, and gases can be dissolved into liquids.

Assuming that we have been breathing air at sea level for some time, our bodies are saturated with nitrogen at sea level pressure. So, all throughout our tissues nitrogen is in solution at 11.76 psi (.8 bar). As long as we stay at sea level, this concentration of nitrogen will not increase or decrease.

Nitrogen & Your Blood

Our blood absorbs nitrogen from the lungs and carries it in liquid solution to our tissues. Once delivered, it simply stays there as nitrogen in solution; it is not used, as is oxygen.

KNOWLEDGE · SKILLS · DIVER DIAMOND · SSI · EQUIPMENT · EXPERIENCE

Boyle's Law

Depth Feet/Metres	ATM	PSI/bar Ambient Pressure	Volume of a Sealed Container	Density of Gas	% N_2	Partial Pressure N_2
0/0	1	14.7/1	1	1x	80%	11.6
33/10	2	29.4/2	1/2	2x	80%	23.2
66/20	3	44.1/3	1/3	3x	80%	34.8
99/30	4	58.8/4	1/4	4x	80%	46.5

Breathing Air Under Water

When we breathe under water, the Air Delivery System supplies air to our lungs at the same pressure as surrounding water (ambient pressure), as described in Section 1. So, when we take a breath at 33 feet (10 metres), for example, the total pressure in our lungs is 29.4 psi (2 bar), or two times sea level pressure.

Under these conditions of increasing pressures another simple law of physics comes into play. Henry's Law states that the amount of a gas which dissolves in a liquid is proportional to the partial pressure of that gas. In other words, the higher the pressure, the more gas that can be dissolved in a liquid. This means that as the pressure of oxygen and nitrogen increases in the lungs, more of each of these gases is absorbed by the blood and then carried to the tissues.

At Depth

At depth, the volume of air in our lungs is the same, but the gas is more dense. Essentially, we breathe more molecules of the gases as we go deeper, and the partial pressure of each gas increases in proportion to the total surrounding pressure. As we continue to descend, the total ambient pressure increases, and so do the partial pressures of oxygen and nitrogen.

Nitrogen Narcosis

High pressure nitrogen has a narcotic effect on humans. It can cause an abnormal sense of euphoria, paranoia, well being, nervousness and a slowing down or dulling of the normal functions of the brain and body. It is not known exactly why nitrogen has this effect, although many scientists liken it to the effect of anesthesia.

Narcosis

There is no time element involved in the onset of narcosis or with relief from it. Symptoms can occur immediately upon arrival at a depth, and will be relieved as soon as the diver moves to a shallower depth—there is no recovery period to speak of. This makes the cure easy—just ascend slowly to a shallower depth.

Symptoms can be very mild at first and increase as the diver goes deeper. When affected by high pressure nitrogen, a diver may have difficulty doing things that would normally be easy, such as reading and interpreting instruments, making decisions, operating a BC correctly or communicating with a buddy. Nitrogen narcosis can cause dizziness or disorientation, and if the diver continues to descend, eventually unconsciousness.

The depth at which symptoms occur cannot be precisely determined. Many divers will not report any recognizable symptoms of narcosis on dives shallower than 60-80 feet (18-24 metres), though, in clinical studies, divers have shown lack of motor coordination and slowed cognitive processing as shallow as 20 feet (6 metres).

Nitrogen narcosis is one of the main reasons it is recommended that recreational divers stay above 100 feet (30 metres). However, with proper training and preparation, deeper dives can be made. See your instructor or SSI about specialized training in deep diving.

Adapting to the Underwater Environment

Buoyancy

As mentioned in Section 1, Archimedes' Principle describes buoyancy and why the Buoyancy Control System is necessary so divers are not constantly fighting tendencies to either float up or sink down. Establishing neutral buoyancy is a matter of balancing many factors, the first of which is compensating for the diver's own personal tendency to either float or sink.

BCS

As discussed in Section 1, the Buoyancy Compensator System is what the diver uses to balance buoyancy factors and adjust for various diving situations.

The individual's body will fall into one of three buoyancy categories:

1. It will have ***positive buoyancy***, or float, if the body is lighter than the same volume of water.

2. It will have ***negative buoyancy***, or sink, if the body weighs more than an equal volume of water.

3. It will have **neutral buoyancy**, or will tend neither to float nor sink, if the body weighs the same as an equal volume of water.

Proper Weighting

Proper weighting is what allows the diver to get under water and begin a descent. With proper weighting achieved, adjustment of buoyancy under water is accomplished by adding air to or subtracting air from the BC.

To properly weight yourself you need to be wearing the weight system and all the other equipment you will have on during the dive.

1. Enter the water and test that you are not greatly overweighted.

2. Move to an area where you are suspended upright in water over your head. Your objective is to be able to float with each inhalation and sink with each exhalation at the surface with the weight system on and the BC deflated.

3. As you inhale, your eyes should rise slightly above the surface; as you exhale, you should sink below the surface, just enough to cover the top of your head.

4. The water level should rise and fall around eye level. Add or remove weight as needed to achieve this. Track your weighting needs in the tables provided in your Total DiveLog.

Controlling Buoyancy Under Water

When neutrally buoyant, you need to exhale to get below the surface and begin your descent feet-first. As divers descend, exposure suit buoyancy is reduced by compression, making the diver negatively buoyant. When your suit loses buoyancy and you begin to sink, add small amounts of air to the BC to compensate, so that you can control the descent.

When you want to stabilize at a depth, add or subtract small amounts of air to the BC until you become suspended. If you feel unbalanced in the water and are leaning too far backward, you may need to move your weights slightly forward to counteract the weight of the cylinder.

Neutrally Buoyant

When you are neutrally buoyant you will rise slightly when you inhale and sink slightly when you exhale.

Once neutrally buoyant at any depth, if you move into shallower water, the air in your BC will expand and you will need to release air from the BC. If you move into deeper water, the air in the BC will compress, causing you to lose buoyancy. You will need to add air to the BC to remain neutrally buoyant.

Being too negative can also lead to difficulty. Becoming mesmerized by the beauty of your surroundings is one thing, but unless you have established neutral buoyancy, the next time you look at your depth gauge you may find that you have unintentionally descended another twenty or thirty feet. Negative buoyancy can also make you constantly work to stay off the bottom and thereby risk overexertion. Negatively buoyant divers also wreak havoc to the substrate and may be injured by unintentionally contacting marine life such as sea urchins.

The Mask

The mask lens, in combination with water and the space behind the lens, makes objects appear to be 25% closer and 33% larger to the diver. This is because light is refracted in the mask before entering the eye and focusing on the retina.

25% Closer
33% Larger

Controlling your buoyancy at depth requires practice, and is a skill you will discover to be essential. Once you have experienced the wonderful feeling of weightless suspension under water and the ease it provides you while diving, you will naturally want to become skillful at maintaining neutral buoyancy.

Vision

Water refracts light differently than air, causing objects to appear out of focus when viewed under water with the naked eye. As discussed in Section 1, one of the beneficial effects of the mask is that it restores the natural medium of air to the area surrounding the eyes, allowing the eyes to focus.

Under water, vision is also affected by turbid water, water with suspended particles such as minerals and organic matter. These particles scatter and absorb light, impairing vision. To learn more about diving in turbid water, ask your SSI Dealer about a Night/Limited Visibility Diving Specialty Course.

Communication

Hand Signals

The most common way divers communicate is by using a number of hand signals devised by the diving community (See pages 3-18 and 3-19). Some divers use slight variations of these signals, so before you dive make sure you go over signals and agree upon the ones you will be using and what they mean.

Normal human communication involves hearing and speaking, but both of these actions are adversely affected by the medium of water. Hearing is affected because sound waves travel about four times faster in water than in air. This makes it difficult to know the direction from which sound is coming. On land, sound travels slowly enough to be heard first by the ear nearest to the source of the sound, and then by the other ear, indicating direction.

In water, sound travels so fast that you usually cannot distinguish the direction of its source.

1. Low on air

2. Out of air

3. Ok?/ Ok.

4. Stop/Hold it/
Stay there

5. Share air

6. Come here

7. Me/Watch me

8. Level off/
This depth

9. Ears not
clearing

10. Go up/
Going up

11. Go down/
Going down

12. Something
is wrong

Clear Communication

Hand signals vary around the world. Before the dive, make sure you and your buddy agree on the hand signals you will use and what they mean.

KNOWLEDGE · SKILLS

DIVER DIAMOND SSI
SCUBA SCHOOLS INTERNATIONAL

EQUIPMENT · EXPERIENCE

13. Go back/ starting point

14. I am cold

15. Question?

16. Ship/ Boat

17. Which direction?

18. Hurry/ Faster

19. Something overhead

20. Distress/ Help (On surface)

21. Ok?/ Ok. (On surface at a distance)

22. Ok?/ Ok. (One hand occupied)

The problem with speaking is that just like vision, speaking is meant to be done in the medium of air. While the vocal folds vibrate and create sound just as on land, the expelled air which carries that sound, in effect, runs into a wall of water. Other sounds, however, are easy to understand as well as hear. You can easily hear a boat motor, for instance, from a long distance.

> ## Talk Underwater?
> Several underwater communication systems are available that enable divers to talk to each other while diving. Many of these systems integrate with the mask and second-stage you already own. The systems are so easy to use all you have to do for your buddy to hear you is talk normally.

A sound all divers need to know is the clanking of a diver's tool or other device against a scuba cylinder. This is a signal to get another diver's attention.

Though speaking under water is nearly impossible, it is still very important to communicate with your buddy and other divers. To "speak" to each other, divers may use a slate and marker, which usually attach to the BC. It is imperative that both of you know the emergency signals.

Exposure — Protection from the Environment

Anyone who swims knows that when you first jump into water, even if it is relatively warm water, it feels cold. The reason for this is that the body operates at 98.6° F (37° C) and the water is usually much less than that. Further, the body loses heat faster in water than it does in air—twenty-five times faster. But it does not take long to "get used to it." What actually happens when you get used to the cold is that blood vessels in the skin are constricted and less blood flows to the surface of the body. This slows down heat loss and works to keep the body warm at its core where heat is more vital. But if the body remains exposed to the water for long, this reduced blood flow will not be enough to keep you warm, and the body will try to generate heat by the muscle contractions called shivering.

If the body is allowed to lose heat continually over a period of time, body temperature will actually begin to drop, shivering will become intense and prolonged and extremities will begin to get numb.

When body temperature is allowed to drop to 95°F (35°C), hypothermia sets in. If allowed to drop to 90°F (32°C), reasoning ability will begin to fail, and any temperature below 90°F (32°C) is life threatening. If you ever begin to shiver while diving, stop the dive, get out of the water and rewarm.

Use your exposure suit components to ensure temperature stability as discussed in Section 1. For example, if you think you might need a hood, go ahead and wear it. It is easier for your body to cool down in a liquid medium than it is to rewarm once it has cooled. Remember, your comfort affects your enjoyment.

Effects of Decreasing Pressure

Whereas increasing pressure decreases the volume of gas, the opposite is also true. Decreasing pressure allows gas to expand.

♦ If you filled a balloon at 66 feet (20 metres) under 3 atmospheres of pressure and then began to ascend, the air inside would expand to three times the volume by the time it reached the surface. Could the balloon hold that volume of air?

♦ Your sinuses and ears will allow air to escape naturally, equalizing as you go, but the diver must consciously allow air to escape the lungs.

♦ It is extremely important for the diver to breathe normally while ascending. As long as you breathe normally, the airway will remain open.

Always breathe normally, never hold your breath. Breathing normally means that when you are not inhaling, you are exhaling, so you are breathing at all times.

◆ Even in the rare case of an emergency when getting to the surface is a priority, the diver must remember to breathe normally so that air can escape the lungs as diminishing outside pressure allows the air inside them to expand. Tilting the head back and looking up will also help keep the airway open.

Overexpansion Injuries

Failure to keep an open airway to the lungs upon ascent can result in one of four overexpansion injuries. If a diver ascends without breathing and instead holds his or her breath, trapped gas in the lungs must find a way to escape.

Air Embolism

◆ When lung tissue ruptures and air bubbles pass into the blood stream, the diver may experience an air embolism.

◆ The blood will carry these air bubbles into smaller arteries until a blockage forms and restricts blood flow. This can happen in various areas of the body, but some air bubbles in the bloodstream may travel to the brain. This can eventually cut off circulation to brain tissue, resulting in the most serious example of an embolism.

Symptoms of air embolism can be as slight as numbness in an arm or leg or a temporary loss of vision, hearing, or speech. Or symptoms can be as serious as paralysis and unconsciousness and may even lead to death.

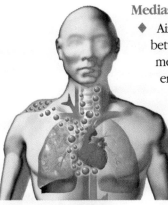

Mediastinal and Subcutaneous Emphysema

◆ Air may also escape a damaged lung into the space between the heart, lungs and windpipe called the mediastinum. This is known as mediastinal emphysema.

   ◆ Air pressure against the heart can cause chest pain, breathing difficulty, and faintness.

   ◆ Bubbles in the mediastinum can also travel up along the windpipe and gather under the skin in the neck or upper chest, resulting in subcutaneous emphysema, a thick, raised rash which can impair speech and breathing if located near the larynx.

Pneumothorax

◆ The lungs are separated from the chest wall by a membrane called the pleural lining.

◆ If air bubbles escape into the space between the lungs and the pleural lining, a pocket of air can form which in an extreme case can collapse the lung when that air expands and squeezes the lung as the diver ascends. This injury is called pneumothorax.

Signs and symptoms of pneumothorax may include shortness of breath and chest pain.

Decompression Sickness

The possibility of decompression sickness is another problem associated with the increased partial pressure of nitrogen to which a diver is exposed when breathing under water.

As the diver descends and the partial pressure of nitrogen breathed into the lungs increases, the blood absorbs this extra nitrogen quite readily and carries it in solution out to the tissues. The tissues then absorb the nitrogen and keep it in solution under pressure.

When the diver moves back into shallower water and the partial pressure of nitrogen drops, the process is reversed. The blood coming from the lungs now has less nitrogen pressure, allowing the tissues to release nitrogen back into the blood, which then carries it back to the lungs where it is exhaled.

During this process of releasing nitrogen from the tissues, it is important that the diver come up slowly enough to allow the nitrogen to stay in solution in the tissues and blood while it is being released.

If the diver ascends too quickly, the nitrogen will come out of solution and form gas bubbles in the tissues and blood which can cause blockages and create symptoms of decompression sickness.

The principle of bubble formation can be demonstrated by a bottle of carbonated beverage with a twist top. When the cap is on, the liquid is clear. There is no indication that the liquid contains a gas because the gas is in solution under pressure. When you twist the cap off, bubbles immediately form in the liquid because of lessening pressure.

In Short

The simplest explanation of what causes decompression sickness is that nitrogen bubbles form in the body when a diver ascends too fast after breathing compressed air under water while too deep for too long.

DCS Symptoms

Depending on where the nitrogen bubble blockages form, a variety of problems can result.

◆ If the bubbles occur in the capillaries near the surface of the skin, an irritable rash may break out.

◆ Breathing difficulty, coughing, and a burning sensation in the chest signal a hit in a lung.

◆ If the blockage forms in a joint or muscle, pain will be felt in that area. Loss of feeling, tingling in the extremities, and/or paralysis indicate a spinal cord hit. Nausea, extreme fatigue and weakness may also occur.

◆ Dizziness, paralysis, temporary blindness, convulsions and unconsciousness may indicate a blockage in the brain.

Symptoms usually appear within 15 minutes to 12 hours after surfacing, but can appear sooner. Delayed occurrence of symptoms is rare but can happen, especially if air travel or driving to higher altitude follows the dive.

First Aid and Treatment

As we discussed earlier, all compressed gas injuries, whether decompression sickness or arterial gas embolism, are treated as decompression illness.

First aid for the decompression illness victim includes breathing as high a concentration of oxygen as is available, 100% if possible.

Keep the victim still, placing him or her in a comfortable position, and if conscious, giving nonalcoholic fluids such as water.

Treatment for decompression sickness is immediate recompression in a hyperbaric chamber.

This reduces the size of the bubbles so that they can go back into solution. The diver is then brought out of pressure slowly enough to allow the nitrogen to be released as it should have been in the first place.

Again, as a precaution, all divers should know how to activate the emergency medical services for the region.

Prevention

When diving, the two factors that determine how much nitrogen you absorb are depth and time.

♦ The deeper you go, the denser the air you breathe and the more nitrogen there is to absorb.

♦ The longer you stay under water, the more time your body has to accumulate nitrogen.

♦ The absorption of nitrogen by the tissues takes time, and it does not occur at the same rate throughout the body.

♦ Some tissues absorb and give off nitrogen very readily while others do so more slowly.

When you return to the surface, you do not need to bring the nitrogen level back to the same 11.76 psi (.8 bar) it was at the beginning of the dive. After a dive, while you are on the surface, you will continue to release nitrogen until you are back to that normal partial pressure at sea level. If you dive again before your nitrogen returns to this level, you have to take your present level into consideration, and so on throughout the day. This will become more clear when you learn how to use your computer and the dive tables in the next section.

The key thing to remember about preventing decompression sickness is returning to the surface slowly enough to allow nitrogen to be released from the blood and tissues without coming out of solution. During this slow ascent your body naturally vents off extra nitrogen.

**15 feet
(4.5 metres)**

I Minute

**45 feet
(14 metres)**

The proper rate of ascent is 30 feet (9 metres) per minute.

If divers surpass recommended time limits at certain depths, they are said to have made a decompression dive and therefore must make a decompression stop before surfacing. A decompression stop is required when a diver has taken on too much nitrogen to vent off during a normal ascent to the surface. Decompression diving is outside the scope of recreational scuba diving and increases the risk of decompression sickness.

Safety Stop!

As an extra safety measure, always make a safety stop of 3-5 minutes at 15 feet (4.5 metres) on any dive over 30 feet (9 metres). The recommended safety stop comes out of the 1989 Biomechanics of Safe Ascents Workshop, which was sponsored by the American Academy of Underwater Sciences. Other countries, such as Japan and Australia, that recommend a 5-minute stop at 16 feet (5 metres) have based this recommendation on studies from their own countries.

Depth and time limits for no-decompression dives are on a chart devised by the U.S. Navy called the U.S. Navy Dive Tables. These tables show divers how to minimize the possibility of decompression sickness.

First Aid for Divers

DCS & Overexpansion

Overexpansion injuries and DCS have such similar symptoms that they should all be treated as decompression illness until such a time as it is determined otherwise.

The current medical thinking describes both overexpansion injuries, including arterial gas embolism (AGE) and decompression sickness (DCS), as decompression illness (DCI) for purposes of treatment. Over-expansion injuries and DCS have such similar symptoms that they should all be treated as decompression illness until such a time as it is determined otherwise. The injured diver will need immediate medical care; therefore, getting proper medical help is your first priority. If possible, the transportation of the victim to a medical facility is best handled by professionals.

Any victim of DCI may require recompression in a hyperbaric chamber, or "recompression chamber" as it is sometimes called.

Asphyxiation occurs when the gas exchange process completely breaks down. When asphyxia occurs in water it can lead to drowning. If someone stops breathing it is very important to get breathing started again by means of artificial respiration, also known as rescue breathing. Unless breathing is restored, the heart will also stop within a few minutes. When this happens, cardiopulmonary re-suscitation (CPR) must be performed.

There are a few precautions all divers should take to be prepared. These may never become necessary but do add an extra measure of security to an already safe activity and a valuable measure of competence to the diver.

> ### Regulator Safety
>
> A poorly tuned or inadequate regulator can also lead to respiratory distress. It is important that you have a regulator designed for the type of diving that you will be doing and that you have it serviced regularly.

♦ **Take a CPR and Rescue Breathing Course.** Rescue breathing and CPR should only be performed by persons who are trained in the techniques. It is recommended that anyone involved in aquatic activities should be CPR trained. SSI recommends an organization called React Right (**www.reactright.com**). Your SSI Training Facility has more information on First Aid and CPR course schedules.

> ### Be Prepared
>
> Being a prepared diver will prevent problems from arising in the first place.

◆ **Know Contact Information.** Know how to contact, from land and boat, the local ambulance, EMS system and/or dive rescue service for the region. Your country may also have a national medical information network for divers. Consult your SSI Instructor.

Write all contact information in your SSI Total DiveLog.

◆ **Know Phone Location.** Locate the telephone nearest to where you are diving and make sure it is accessible.

◆ **Recognize Stress.** Watch for erratic behavior in your buddy, and be aware of signs of stress in yourself. Obvious signs of stress under water are rapid, shallow breathing and a wide-eyed expression. If signs of stress are present, stop, breathe normally and think. If necessary, make a proper ascent to the surface with your buddy.

The prevention of panic in a stressful situation by calm, corrective action is much easier and more effective than dealing with a panicked diver. During SSI's Diver Stress and Rescue training, you learn how to deal with these problems.

◆ **Alert Others, Get Help.** If a diver is injured or ill, alert other people in the area. Whether you are on land or in the water, call for help and get others to assist you in caring for the victim. You must assist the victim until professional medical help arrives.

◆ **Get Victim Out of the Water.** If you are in the water, get the victim onto the shore or deck as soon as possible. Efforts to perform rescue breathing or first aid while in the water may interfere with the quickest possible removal of the victim from the water.

While it is important to know emergency precautions, properly trained divers who use good judgement should never need to use them or make it necessary for others to use them.

To review, before transport to a medical facility, or until professional medical attention is available, the victim must be stabilized:

◆ Remove the injured person from danger.

◆ Manage the ABC's of basic life support.

◆ Provide 100% oxygen.

◆ Activate the local emergency medical system (EMS) immediately. (Know the phone numbers for the local EMS).

◆ If the diver has serious symptoms and has breathed under water, CPR or rescue breathing with the highest possible concentration of oxygen may be necessary.

Part of being a buddy is being responsive to your buddy's needs in any situation. Being a good athlete or a comfortable diver or even a helpful dive partner does not necessarily make you a good buddy. Being a buddy not only takes competence and caring, it takes responsibility. If you and your buddy are not familiar with basic first-aid and rescue techniques, it is a good idea to take a React Right First-aid and CPR course and an SSI Diver Stress and Rescue course. The SSI Diver Stress and Rescue course will teach you how to prevent, detect and manage diver stress and possible rescue situations. Your SSI Instructor and Dealer have all the information you will need to enroll in one or both of these courses.

Ascent Procedures

All it takes to avoid overexpansion problems is breathing normally and following correct ascent procedures. Get into the habit of using these procedures every time you ascend, regardless of depth.

Normal Ascents:

1. Check with your buddy, making sure you are both ready to ascend, then plan to ascend together.

2. Place in view any instruments you are using to keep track of your rate of ascent. Go slowly in any normal ascent.

3. Hold the inflator hose upright in your left hand with the arm extended and vent air from the BC as needed to control your ascent. This will also keep one arm positioned above to warn you of possible obstructions overhead.

4. Facing your buddy, look toward the surface and select a clear path.

5. While neutrally buoyant, start your ascent by kicking gently upward. Periodically look upward to see what is above you and to check on your buddy's position.

6. Ascend at the rate of 30 feet (9 metres) per minute or less. You can keep track of your rate of ascent by monitoring your instruments.

7. Make a safety stop at 15 feet (4.5 metres) for 3-5 minutes.

8. Breathe normally and continuously all the way to the surface. Again, never hold your breath. Also, do not remove the regulator until after you have surfaced and inflated your BC.

9. When you reach the surface inflate the BC, do a weight system check (rehearsing what you would do if you needed to ditch the system), keep your mask in place, and either keep the regulator in place or switch to snorkel breathing.

Air Sharing

Though it is unlikely you will ever run out of air, you must nevertheless be prepared for the possibility of an out-of-air situation.

When talking about air sharing we refer to the buddy who needs air as the needer and the buddy who assists as the donor.

If a diver is having an air supply problem and a buddy is nearby, the needer would give the buddy, the donor, the hand signals for "out of air" and "let's share air." At that time the buddy would react in one of several ways depending on the exact circumstances. The primary concerns would be to

"Out of Air"

♦ Get the needer an air source and

♦ Surface safely.

Alternate Air Sharing Ascents

After being alerted by the needer, the donor should take control of the situation, offering the most immediately available air source.

"Let's Share Air"

♦ If the donor is equipped with an alternate air source such as an inflator-integrated air source, he or she should offer the primary second-stage to the needer and then locate the alternate air source to breathe from.

♦ If the donor is equipped with an alternate second-stage regulator, the donor has the option to pass either the primary regulator or the alternate second- stage regulator.

♦ If either the donor or the needer is equipped with an independent air source, the needer can breathe from it while the donor breathes from the primary second-stage.

After breathing is under control, the donor and needer have to establish a physical link:

◆ Hook the right arms together and holding onto each other's BCs or BC shoulder straps, keeping the left arms of both divers free to control the inflators while ascending.

◆ The donor determines when both divers are ready to ascend.

◆ The divers should make a controlled ascent together.

An air sharing situation will rarely, if ever, arise in recreational diving. But by knowing and practicing the skills, you add an extra element of confidence to your experience as a diver.

Emergency Ascents

What if you have a problem with your air supply, are low on air, or out of air, and no one is there to help? Your only option would be to get to the surface quickly.

There are two methods for ascending in an emergency:

◆ The emergency swimming ascent

◆ The emergency buoyant ascent.

First and foremost when talking about emergency ascents is the importance of maintaining proper buoyancy. Any time a diver needs to get to the surface quickly, an ascent is easiest to initiate when the diver is already at least neutral or slightly positive.

Alternate Air

Always know the placement and type of alternate air source your buddy is using. Always do a predive check for the alternate air source location and discuss the sharing air procedure.

KNOWLEDGE · SKILLS · EQUIPMENT · EXPERIENCE

DIVER DIAMOND SSI

It is very important to get into the habit of maintaining neutral buoyancy at all times while diving.

Emergency Swimming Ascent

If the diver becomes aware of being low on air, or has some other air supply problem which has not entirely shut off the air, he or she will be able to swim to the surface.

An emergency swimming ascent is essentially the same as a normal ascent except that you are prepared to ditch your weight system for immediate positive buoyancy if necessary.

To make an emergency swimming ascent:

1. Keep your second-stage in your mouth.

2. Hold your weight system release with the right hand.

3. Kick toward the surface, and vent air from the BC to control your ascent.

4. Try to maintain a slow ascent rate.

The reason for being poised to ditch the weights is that in many diving accidents the diver successfully reaches the surface, only to sink back down into the water. Fatalities have occurred because of this. This leads us to the main objective of the emergency buoyant ascent.

Emergency Buoyant Ascent

The emergency buoyant ascent is done in the case of a sudden loss of air which requires an immediate return to the surface. To perform the emergency buoyant ascent:

1. Keep your second-stage in your mouth.

2. Immediately ditch the weight system at depth, utilizing the quick draw method. (Hold the weights away from your body and then drop them.) This provides positive buoyancy, which begins lifting the diver. From depths beyond which the wet suit has lost its buoyancy, a gentle kick will assist the ascent.

3. Vent air from the lungs by continuously exhaling.

4. Stay relaxed, keep the head back & look up.

5. Hold the inflator hose aloft in the left hand, and let air escape the BC during the ascent if necessary.

6. Flare the body and stop kicking in the last 20 feet (6 metres) or so to slow the ascent when approaching the surface. To flare as you approach the surface, lay back in the water and spread your arms and legs.

The advantage of the buoyant ascent is that it assures the diver of surfacing, and the knowledge of this fact may even lessen the diver's worries.

Only opt for surfacing if there is no way to solve a problem under water. With any ascent, only surface faster than 30 feet (9 metres) per minute when absolutely necessary; remember that you are risking overexpansion and/or decompression problems by ascending faster than 30 feet (9 metres) per minute.

It is recommended that you always locate the weight system and mentally rehearse ditching it after you surface, every time you dive. Unlike normal diving skills, emergency skills need to be learned despite the fact that you may never use them. You need to learn these skills not just by reading about them but by mentally rehearsing them every time you dive so that they will be second nature in case you ever do need them. An annual skills update is also highly recommended. See your SSI Dealer about taking a Scuba Skills Update course.

Cover Your Bases

If you are confused or panicked and there is a doubt about which ascent to use, ditch the weights and do the buoyant ascent. This covers all your bases and

◆ You will surface,

◆ You will stay on the surface.

Summary

This section is full of technical information, possible hazards, and emergency and first aid advice. Do not let it overwhelm you or lead you to believe that you have gotten yourself in over your head, so to speak. It still holds that diving is easy and fun when a properly trained and equipped diver performs the skills properly. There is no mystery, just knowledge and practice. Diving injuries and fatalities usually happen because of lack of training, poor judgement, divers exceeding personal limits of skill level or physical capacity or panic. Seldom do accidents occur for no preventable or avoidable reason. Basic knowledge of your physiology and the physics of diving will help you develop proper behaviors and an informed attitude that will keep you and your buddy out of trouble under water.

Section 3 Study Guide Questions

1. Ear equalization, or "clearing," should be _____ _____ upon descending and continued as you dive deeper, and should never be done _____.

2. If your sinuses are blocked, it is best not to _____ until the problem is _____ and they are open again.

3. A common reaction to anxiety or fear is a _____, _____ breathing pattern.

4. Unless a diver _____, _____ and gets _____ under control, stress, and even panic may result.

5. To prevent carbon dioxide excess, avoid _____ and dive with high quality, well maintained _____.

6. Always breathe _____, never hold your breath; even if the _____ is out of your mouth while under water, develop a habit of _____ a steady stream of bubbles.

7. Proper weighting is what allows the diver to get under water and begin a descent. With proper weighting achieved, adjustment of _____ under water is accomplished by _____ air to or _____ air from the BC.

8. Once neutrally buoyant at any depth, if you move into _____ water, the air in your BC will expand and you will need to _____ air from the BC until you become suspended.

9. Hearing is affected (underwater) because soundwaves travel about _____ times faster in water than in air.

10. A sound all divers need to know is the clanking of a diver's tool or other device against a _____ _____. This is a signal to get another diver's attention.

11. The body loses heat faster in water than it does in air— _____ times faster.

12. When body temperature is allowed to drop to 95 F (35 C), _____ sets in.

13. Failure to keep an open airway to the lungs upon ascent can result in one of four _____ injuries.

14. During the process of releasing nitrogen from the tissues, it is important that the diver comes up _____ enough to allow the _____ to stay in solution in the tissues and blood while it is being released.

15. The proper rate of ascent is _____, per minute.

16. Write all contact information in your _____ _____ _____.

17. While it is important to know emergency precautions, _____ _____ divers who use good _____ should never need to use them, or make it necessary for others to use them.

18. After your ascent, when you reach the surface, inflate the _____, do a weight system check, keep your _____ in place, and either keep the _____ in place or switch to snorkel breathing.

19. An emergency _____ ascent is essentially the same as a normal ascent except that you are prepared to ditch your weight system for immediate positive buoyancy if necessary.

20. If you are confused or panicked and there is doubt about which ascent to use, ditch the weights and do the _____ ascent.

Planning and Executing Your Dive

"Tread softly, for this is holy ground. It may be, could we look with seeing eyes, this spot we stand on is paradise."

— Christine Rosetti

For your comfort and enjoyment, there are many reasons for planning and executing your dive according to your plan. Among the most essential is avoiding decompression sickness.

As you learned in previous sections, divers breathing air under pressure will absorb nitrogen from the air they breathe. The deeper we go, the longer we stay at depth, and the more dives we make in a single day, the more nitrogen our bodies may absorb.

To avoid decompression sickness, some of the nitrogen you take in during your dives must be breathed off during your ascent. If a diver goes too deep and/or stays too long, either on a single dive or a series of dives, the nitrogen level can get so high in the body that the diver cannot return directly to the surface, even by ascending slowly, without making a stop or multiple stops on the way up. This is known as decompression diving and is to be avoided in recreational diving. The recreational diver's goal is to plan dives so that he or she is always free to ascend slowly, but directly, to the surface without risking decompression sickness. This is called no-decompression diving.

Section 4 Objectives

After completing this section you will understand

♦ Why divers need to use SSI Dive Tables or a dive computer on every dive,

♦ How the SSI Dive Tables work,

♦ Common dive computer features and functions,

♦ The benefit of owning and using a dive computer,

♦ How other factors can affect nitrogen absorption and decompression,

♦ The value of diving with a buddy and buddy team functioning and

♦ How to execute your dive.

To avoid decompression sickness, always ascend slowly, no faster than 30 feet (9 metres)/minute, and plan your dives according to the no-decompression limits of the SSI Dive Tables or a dive computer. As an added safety measure, stop at 15 feet (4.5 metres) for 3-5 minutes on every ascent.

How deep? How long? How often? We have two methods to answer these questions in diving, the SSI Dive Tables and dive computers. Both methods are based on various mathematical models representing theories of tissue absorption, tolerance and release of nitrogen.

The SSI Dive Tables are derived from Doppler Bubble tests performed by the U.S. Navy. They are designed for dives in which the diver descends to a maximum depth and remains at that depth for the entire dive. Since most recreational dives are multi-level dives, one of the most welcome advantages of dive computers is that they respond to changing depths and are continually recalculating during a dive. The result on most dives is more time under water without needing a decompression stop.

There are many excellent dive computers on the market, from basic to advanced, with an impressive list of features and capabilities.

Under water, computers are your depth indicator and bottom timer. During the dive, they will tell you how long you can stay at the depth you are without needing a decompression stop. To avoid getting into decompression, you simply move into shallower water as the remaining bottom time indicates. During ascent, your computer will warn you if you are ascending too quickly. While you are on the surface, the computer will continue to calculate nitrogen release, so when you make a second dive, it is including calculations of nitrogen still in your body from the previous dive(s).

Many dive computers also include functions that compensate automatically for diving at altitude, and they calculate the best amount of time you should wait before flying after diving based on your dive profiles.

More information on computer functions is given later in this section. Your SSI Dealer and Instructor are available to help you choose the computer that is right for you and the type of diving you will be doing.

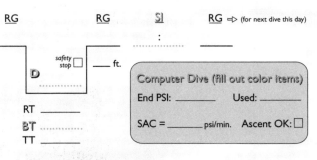

Dive Planning

The Dive Profile

Dive computers and the dive tables are designed to allow you to make as many repetitive dives per day as you would like, as long as you remain within the no-decompression limits. To keep track of multiple dives, divers use a dive profile. In most cases, this will be a simple graph that includes all the relevant information for recording no-decompression and repetitive dives. The type of profile you use will depend on the use of a dive table or a dive computer. Consult your computer's user manual for information on its dive profile display. Regardless of what you are using, dive tables or a dive computer, you and your buddy should always complete the dive profile provided in your SSI Total DiveLog System.

Dive Tables and Terminology

Though diving with a computer is the method of choice for most divers today, it is important that you understand how the SSI Dive Tables work to plan a dive or a series of dives. Before we begin to explain the dive tables, we must all speak the same language, or use the same terminology. Listed below are some of the key terms you must know in order to help you better understand how to use the dive tables.

1. **Bottom Time (BT).** The amount of elapsed time from the start of your descent to the time you begin your direct ascent back to the surface.

2. **Decompression Dive.** A dive that exceeds no-decompression time limits, thus requiring planned decompression stops to eliminate excess nitrogen accumulated during the dive. Note: Decompression diving is beyond the scope of this course and is not considered part of recreational diving.

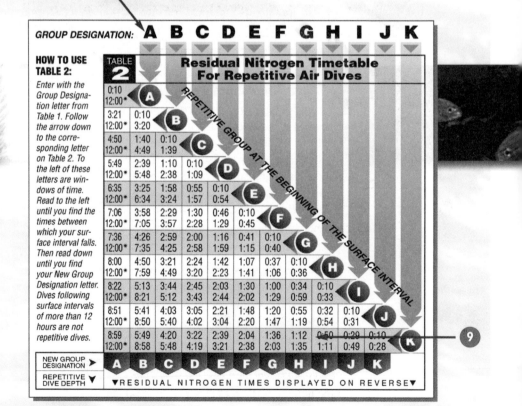

TABLE 1 — No-Decompression Limits and Repetitive Group Designation Table For No-Decompression Air Dives

HOW TO USE TABLE 1: Find the planned depth of your dive in feet or metres at the far left of Table 1. Read to the right until you find the time (minutes) you plan to spend at that depth. Read down to find the Group Designation letter.

DEPTH feet / metres	Doppler No-Decompression Limits (minutes)	A	B	C	D	E	F	G	H	I	J	K
10 / 3.0		60	120	210	300							
15 / 4.5		35	70	110	160	225	350					
20 / 6.0		25	50	75	100	135	180	240	325			
25 / 7.5	245	20	35	55	75	100	125	160	195	245		
30 / 9.0	205	15	30	45	60	75	95	120	145	170	205	
35 / 10.5	160	5	15	25	40	50	60	80	100	120	140	160
40 / 12.0	130	5	15	25	30	40	50	70	80	100	110	130
50 / 15.0	70			10	15	25	30	40	50	60	70	
60 / 18.0	50			10	15	20	25	30	40	50		
70 / 21.0	40			5	10	15	20	30	35	40		
80 / 24.0	30			5	10	15	20	25	30			
90 / 27.0	25			5	10	12	15	20	25			
100 / 30.0	20			5	7	10	15	20				
110 / 33.0	15				5	10	13	15				
120 / 36.0	10				5	10						
130 / 39.0	5				5							

GROUP DESIGNATION: **A B C D E F G H I J K**

GROUP DESIGNATION: **A B C D E F G H I J K**

HOW TO USE TABLE 2:

Enter with the Group Designation letter from Table 1. Follow the arrow down to the corresponding letter on Table 2. To the left of these letters are windows of time. Read to the left until you find the times between which your surface interval falls. Then read down until you find your New Group Designation letter. Dives following surface intervals of more than 12 hours are not repetitive dives.

TABLE 2 — Residual Nitrogen Timetable For Repetitive Air Dives

REPETITIVE GROUP AT THE BEGINNING OF THE SURFACE INTERVAL

0:10 / 12:00*	**A**										
3:21 / 12:00*	0:10 / 3:20	**B**									
4:50 / 12:00*	1:40 / 4:49	0:10 / 1:39	**C**								
5:49 / 12:00*	2:39 / 5:48	1:10 / 2:38	0:10 / 1:09	**D**							
6:35 / 12:00*	3:25 / 6:34	1:58 / 3:24	0:55 / 1:57	0:10 / 0:54	**E**						
7:06 / 12:00*	3:58 / 7:05	2:29 / 3:57	1:30 / 2:28	0:46 / 1:29	0:10 / 0:45	**F**					
7:36 / 12:00*	4:26 / 7:35	2:59 / 4:25	2:00 / 2:58	1:16 / 1:59	0:41 / 1:15	0:10 / 0:40	**G**				
8:00 / 12:00*	4:50 / 7:59	3:21 / 4:49	2:24 / 3:20	1:42 / 2:23	1:07 / 1:41	0:37 / 1:06	0:10 / 0:36	**H**			
8:22 / 12:00*	5:13 / 8:21	3:44 / 5:12	2:45 / 3:43	2:03 / 2:44	1:30 / 2:02	1:00 / 1:29	0:34 / 0:59	0:10 / 0:33	**I**		
8:51 / 12:00*	5:41 / 8:50	4:03 / 5:40	3:05 / 4:02	2:21 / 3:04	1:48 / 2:20	1:20 / 1:47	0:55 / 1:19	0:32 / 0:54	0:10 / 0:31	**J**	
8:59 / 12:00*	5:49 / 8:58	4:20 / 5:48	3:22 / 4:19	2:39 / 3:21	2:04 / 2:38	1:36 / 2:03	1:12 / 1:35	0:50 / 1:11	0:29 / 0:49	0:10 / 0:28	**K**

NEW GROUP DESIGNATION ▶	A B C D E F G H I J K
REPETITIVE DIVE DEPTH ▼	▼RESIDUAL NITROGEN TIMES DISPLAYED ON REVERSE▼

TABLE 3 — Residual Nitrogen Times (Minutes)

— CONTINUED FROM REVERSE SIDE —

=ADJUSTED NO-DECOMPRESSION TIME LIMITS   N/L=NO LIMIT

REPETITIVE DIVE DEPTH feet	metres	A	B	C	D	E	F	G	H	I	J	K
10	3	39 / N/L	88 / N/L	159 / N/L	279 / N/L							
20	6	18 / N/L	39 / N/L	62 / N/L	88 / N/L	120 / N/L	159 / N/L	208 / N/L	279 / N/L	399 / N/L		
30	9	12 / 193	25 / 180	39 / 166	54 / 151	70 / 135	88 / 117	109 / 96	132 / 73	159 / 46	190 / 15	
40	12	7 / 123	17 / 113	25 / 105	37 / 93	49 / 81	61 / 69	73 / 57	87 / 43	101 / 29	116 / 14	
50	15	6 / 64	13 / 57	21 / 49	29 / 41	38 / 32	47 / 23	56 / 14	66 / 4			
60	18	5 / 45	11 / 39	17 / 33	24 / 26	30 / 20	36 / 14	44 / 6				
70	21	4 / 36	9 / 31	15 / 25	20 / 20	26 / 14	31 / 9	37 / 3				
80	24	4 / 26	8 / 22	13 / 17	18 / 12	23 / 7	28 / 2					
90	27	3 / 22	7 / 18	11 / 14	16 / 9	20 / 5	24 / 1					
100	30	3 / 17	7 / 13	10 / 10	14 / 6	18 / 2						
110	33	3 / 13	6 / 9	10 / 5	13 / 2							
120	36	3 / 7	6 / 4	9 / 1								
130	39	3 / 2										

HOW TO USE TABLE 3: Enter with the New Group Designation letter from Table 2. Next, find the planned depth of your repetitive dive in feet or metres at the far left of Table 3. The box that intersects the Repetitive Dive Depth and the New Group Designation will have two numbers. The top number indicates the Residual Nitrogen Time. The bottom number indicates the maximum Adjusted No-Decompression Time Limit for the next dive.

RG — RG — SI : — RG ⇨ (for next dive this day)

safety stop ☐ _____ ft.

D

RT _____

BT

TT _____

Computer Dive (fill out color items)

End PSI: _____   Used: _____

SAC = _____ psi/min.   Ascent OK: ☐

3. **Depth.** The deepest point reached during the dive, no matter how briefly you stayed there. This means that even if you had only planned to go to 30 feet (9 metres), but you became interested in an artifact lying at 40 feet (12 metres) and go to investigate it—even briefly—the depth you use in calculating your dive is 40 feet (12 metres).

4. **Doppler Limits.** More conservative recommended no-decompression time limits at depth than the U.S. Navy time limits, based on Doppler Ultrasound Research.

5. **Group Designation Letter.** The letter assigned after a dive which indicates the amount of residual nitrogen remaining in the diver's tissues.

6. **No-Decompression Dive.** Any dive that can be made to a certain depth for a maximum amount of time so that a direct ascent can be made to the surface; a dive that does not require decompression stops in order to reduce excess nitrogen.

7. **Repetitive Dive.** Any dive started more than 10 minutes and less than 12 hours after a previous scuba dive.

8. **Residual Time (RT).** Excessive nitrogen pressure still residual in the diver at the beginning of a repetitive dive, expressed as minutes of exposure at the planned repetitive dive depth. On your first dive you have zero residual time because you have not yet completed a dive.

9. **Surface Interval (SI).** The amount of time the diver stays out of the water or on the surface between dives, beginning as soon as the diver surfaces and ending at the start of the next descent.

10. **Total Time (TT).** The time divers must use to calculate their new repetitive group designation at the end of a repetitive dive. Calculated as Bottom Time (BT) + Residual Time (RT) = Total Time (TT).

TABLE 1:
The No-Decompression Limits Table

The first function of Table 1, No-Decompression Limits and Repetitive Group Designation Table for No-Decompression Air Dives, which we refer to as the No-Decompression Limits table, is to show divers how long they can stay at certain depths before taking in too much nitrogen to make a direct return to the surface. The set limits are shown on the upper, rectangular shaped portion of the table. If you do not find the exact time in the table, round up to the next greater time.

The two columns on the left show depth in feet and metres. The next column over shows the Doppler No-Decompression

TABLE 1	No-Deco Designati	
DEPTH feet / metres		**Doppler No-Decompression Limits (minutes)**
10	3.0	
15	4.5	
20	6.0	
25	7.5	245
30	9.0	205
35	10.5	(160)
40	12.0	130
50	15.0	(70)
60	18.0	50

Table 1

While the Doppler No-Decompression Limits refer to the maximum time you can spend at certain depths, the numbers to the right of these columns correspond to the time you actually spend diving. In other words, you would rarely dive for the maximum of 205 minutes at 30 feet (9 metres) just because that is the no-decompression limit. For example, you may more likely dive 30 feet (9 metres) for only 35 minutes.

Limits in minutes. You cross reference these numbers to find the maximum number of minutes you can spend at these depths. For example, if you are diving to a depth of 35 feet (10.5 metres), your maximum no-decompression limit at that depth is 160 minutes. If you are diving to 50 feet (15 metres), your maximum no-decompression time at that depth is 70 minutes, and so forth.

Now, it is unlikely that you would ever dive to a certain depth and remain exactly at that depth the entire dive. So, if the deepest point of your dive exceeds a certain No-Decompression Table depth you have planned for, go to the next greater number on the table. For instance, if you had planned to go to 50 feet (15 metres) and the deepest point you reach on your dive is actually 52 feet (16 metres), you refer to 60 (18) on the table.

The next step in using the tables is to find your maximum allowable bottom time at that depth. Using the same example, if you dive to 52 feet (16 metres), refer to 60 (18) on the table and then move to the right and find your Doppler limit at that depth. It is 50 minutes. So, for a dive to 52 feet (16 metres), your maximum bottom time at that depth is 50 minutes. Recall that your bottom time starts when you descend and ends when you begin your direct ascent.

The letter designations you see at the bottom of Table 1 are used to indicate the diver's residual nitrogen after a dive. Every diver has a certain amount of dissolved nitrogen left in his or her body after each dive. This group designation letter is used by the diver to figure out how long a surface interval must be taken before making another dive; that is, how long the diver must stay out of the water before diving again.

TABLE 1	No-Deco Designati
DEPTH feet / metres	Doppler No-Decompression Limits (minutes)

DEPTH feet	DEPTH metres	Doppler No-Decompression Limits (minutes)
10	3.0	
15	4.5	
20	6.0	
25	7.5	245
30	9.0	205
35	10.5	160
40	12.0	130
50	15.0	70
(60)	18.0	(50)

GROUP DESIGNATION:	A	B	C	D	E	F	G	H	I	J	K

Let's continue with our original example of a dive to 52 feet (16 metres) for 36 minutes. You would move in the 60 foot (18 metre) depth bar to the entry for 36 minutes. Because there is no 36 minute limit, you must refer to the next greater time limit which is 40 minutes. Now read straight down. You will see that the group designation for this cross reference is group "G." So, if you make a dive to 52 feet (16 metres) for 36 minutes, which rounds up to a 60 foot (18 metre) dive for 40 minutes, you are said to be a "G-Diver".

TABLE 1	No-Decompression Limits and Rep Designation Table For No-Decompres								
DEPTH feet / metres	Doppler No-Decompression Limits (minutes)	**HOW TO USE TABLE 1:** Find the planned depth at the far left of Table 1. Read to the right until you plan to spend at that depth. Read down to find the							
10 3.0		60	120	210	300			
15 4.5		35	70	110	160	225	350	
20 6.0		25	50	75	100	135	180	240
25 7.5	245	20	35	55	75	100	125	160
30 9.0	205	15	30	45	60	75	95	120
35 10.5	160	5	15	25	40	50	60	80
40 12.0	130	5	15	25	30	40	50	70
50 15.0	70		10	15	25	30	40	50
(60) 18.0	50		10	15	20	25	30	(40)
70 21.0	40		5	10	15	20	30	35
80 24.0	30		5	10	15	20	25	30
90 27.0	25		5	10	12	15	20	25
100 30.0	20		5	7	10	15	20	
110 33.0	15			5	10	13	15	
120 36.0	10			5	10			
130 39.0	5			5				
GROUP DESIGNATION:		**A**	**B**	**C**	**D**	**E**	**F**	(**G**)

RG _____   RG   SI   RG ⇨ (for next dive this day)

G

:

safety stop ☐ __ ft.

D 52

Computer Dive (fill out color items)

End PSI: _____   Used: _____

RT ⓪

BT 36

TT 36

SAC = _____ psi/min.   Ascent OK: ☐

TABLE 2: The Surface Interval Table

For most divers it is just not enough to dive once and then call off your dive day. In fact, scuba diving can be so captivating that it can sometimes seem like an imposition to have to return to the surface at all.

Staying down over certain time limits is not safe, but it is comforting to know that you can safely build into your dive plan what are called repetitive dives.

When planning repetitive dives, refer to the triangle shaped part of the Table which is headed Table 2: Residual Nitrogen Timetable for Repetitive Air Dives. We refer to this table as the Surface Interval Table. This is where your group designation becomes useful.

If your surface interval is less than ten minutes, you must consider both dives to be one continuous dive. If you are out of the water for twelve hours or longer, you are no longer subject to residual times. Dives following surface intervals of less than ten minutes or more than twelve hours are not repetitive dives.

You will notice in Table 2 that the group letters descend in order down the diagonal border of the table. To the left of these diagonal letter designations are various "windows" of time, such as 1 hour and 16 minutes to 1 hour and 59 minutes, or 1:16-1:59, which is located three windows to the left of the letter "G." Your Surface Interval Time (SI), or your time spent out of the water between dives, will lie within one of these time windows.

Assume that you and your buddy decide to stay out of the water for around an hour and a half—time enough to have lunch and refill cylinders. Your surface interval, then, would be 1:30.

Using Table 2, move from your "Group G" designation to the left until you find the times between which one hour and thirty minutes lies. That would be 1:16-1:59. Now notice that while this time frame lies inside a horizontal bar, it is also part of a vertical column which drops down to another set of letters. These letters are aligned across the top of the lower part of Table 2, and the top of Table 3 which is on the back of your dive slate. To figure your residual time, follow down the column from your surface interval time. This will lead you to a new group designation letter, in this case "E".

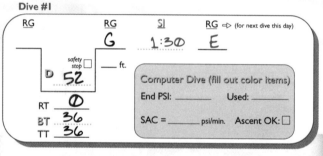

TABLE 3: The Residual Nitrogen Times Table

The rationale behind Table 3, which we refer to as the Residual Nitrogen Times Table, is that even after a surface interval you still retain some nitrogen in your blood and tissues which has not yet come back out of solution. This excess, stored nitrogen in your body is referred to as residual nitrogen, and it requires you to factor in a time deficit when planning your next dive.

You need to plan your next dive as if you have already been under water for a period of time, already taking on nitrogen.

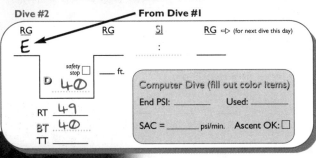

TABLE **3**	**Residual Nitroge** — CONTINUED FRC				
NEW GROUP DESIGNATION ▶	**A**	**B**	**C**	**D**	**E**
REPETITIVE DIVE DEPTH					=ADJUSTED NO-DECOMPR

feet	metres					
10	3	39 N/L	88 N/L	159 N/L	279 N/L	
20	6	18 N/L	39 N/L	62 N/L	88 N/L	120 N/L
30	9	12 193	25 180	39 166	54 151	70 135
⑩40	12	7 123	17 113	25 105	37 93	㊾49 81

Dive #2   **From Dive #1**

RG   RG   SI   RG ⇨ (for next dive this day)

E   :   ____

safety stop ☐ ____ ft.

D 4⓪

Computer Dive (fill out color items)

End PSI: _____   Used: _____

RT 49

BT 4⓪   SAC = _____ psi/min.   Ascent OK: ☐

TT _____

Let's say you would like to make your next dive to 40 feet (12 metres) for somewhere around 40 minutes. You will need to look at the left column of Table 3 where it says "Repetitive Dive Depth" and read for 40 feet (12 metres). Now cross-reference to your new "E-Diver" column. You will find two numbers in this box, 49 and 81. The 49 minutes is your residual time (RT), the time you must assume you have already been absorbing nitrogen at that depth on your second dive. The 81 minutes is your adjusted no-decompression limit, or the total amount of time the Doppler no-decompression limits will allow you to spend at 40 feet (12 metres). Your dive must be less than 81 minutes. This adjusted bottom time has only been calculated for the Doppler limits.

Repetitive Dives and the Dive Profile

Use the profile to record the depth, bottom time and repetitive group from your first dive. After your second dive to 40 feet (12 metres) for 40 minutes, chances are you will want to go down yet again. In this case you will have to come up with another group designation from which you can figure residual time and plan your third dive. Do this by adding your actual bottom time of 40 minutes (which is the bottom time from your second dive) to your residual time of 49 minutes (which we calculated from Table 3 after your first dive) to come up with a total bottom time of 89 minutes. Remember the calculation BT + RT = TT. For this dive your bottom time is then 89 minutes.

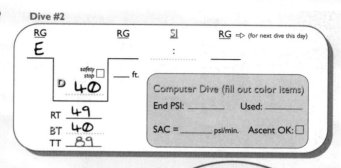

Dive #2

RG   RG   SI   RG ⇨ (for next dive this day)

E

safety stop ☐ ___ ft.

D **4⊘**

RT **49**
BT **4⊘**
TT **89**

Computer Dive (fill out color items)
End PSI: _____   Used: _____
SAC = _____ psi/min.   Ascent OK: ☐

Returning to Table 1, the No-Decompression Table, move from your depth of 40 feet (12 metres) horizontally across to the next greater number above 89 minutes, which is 100 minutes. This gives you a group designation of "I."

Table Use

If you plan deeper dives followed by shallower dives, and keep the depths of your repetitive dives moderate, you will allow yourself longer bottom times and shorter surface intervals in general. It can be annoying and can really limit the day's activities if you use the tables unwisely.

TABLE 1	No-Decompression Limits and R Designation Table For No-Decompr										
DEPTH feet / metres	Doppler No-Decompression Limits (minutes)	HOW TO USE TABLE 1: Find the planned depth o at the far left of Table 1. Read to the right until you fin plan to spend at that depth. Read down to find the Group									
10 3.0		60	120	210	300						
15 4.5		35	70	110	160	225	350				
20 6.0		25	50	75	100	135	180	240	325		
25 7.5	245	20	35	55	75	100	125	160	195	245	
30 9.0	205	15	30	45	60	75	95	120	145	170	
35 10.5	160	5	15	25	40	50	60	80	100	120	
ⓐ40 12.0	130	5	15	25	30	40	50	70	80	ⓞ100	
50 15.0	70		10	15	25	30	40	50	60	70	
60 18.0	50		10	15	20	25	30	40	50		
70 21.0	40		5	10	15	20	30	35	40		
80 24.0	30		5	10	15	20	25	30			
90 27.0	25		5	10	12	15	20	25			
100 30.0	20		5	7	10	15	20				
110 33.0	15			5	10	13	15				
120 36.0	10			5	10						
130 39.0	5			5							

GROUP DESIGNATION: **A B C D E F G H Ⓘ**

Dive #2

RG   RG   SI   RG ⇨ (for next dive this day)

E   **I**

safety stop ☐ ___ ft.

D **4⊘**

RT **49**
BT **4⊘**
TT **89**

Computer Dive (fill out color items)
End PSI: _____   Used: _____
SAC = _____ psi/min.   Ascent OK: ☐

TABLE 2 ▼F ▼G ▼H ⓘ

il Nitrogen Timetabl
epetitive Air Dives

Ⓔ				
0:10 0:45	Ⓕ			
0:41 1:15	0:10 0:40	Ⓖ		
1:07 1:41	0:37 1:06	0:10 0:36	Ⓗ	
(1:30) (2:02)	1:00 1:29	0:34 0:59	0:10 0:33	ⓘ
1:48 2:20	1:20 1:47	0:55 1:19	0:32 0:54	0:10 0:31
2:04 2:38	1:36 2:03	1:12 1:35	0:50 1:11	0:29 0:49
Ⓕ	Ⓖ	Ⓗ	ⓘ	Ⓙ

Again, go to Table 2, the Surface Interval Table, and follow the procedure for determining your surface interval and new group designation. Let's see what would happen if you used the same surface interval as last time—one hour and thirty minutes. Cross-reference from your group letter "I" to the time window 1:30-2:02. Then move down to your new designation as an "F-Diver."

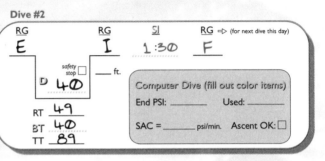

Dive #2

RG — E

RG — I

SI — 1:30

RG — F ⇨ (for next dive this day)

D 40   safety stop ☐ ___ ft.

RT 49
BT 40
TT 89

Computer Dive (fill out color items)
End PSI: _____   Used: _____
SAC = _____ psi/min.   Ascent OK: ☐

Now go to Table 3, the RT Table. If you wanted to go down to 20 feet (6 metres) on a third dive, you would notice on the RT Table that there is no adjusted no-decompression time limit in the 20 foot (6 metre) box. That is because there is not any set no-decompression time limit for 10 or 20 feet (3 or 6 metres). You may also have noticed this in Table 1 under the column "Doppler No-Decompression Limits (minutes)." You will again notice that there is no set limit for 10, 15 or 20 feet (3, 4.5 or 6 metres). These depths are considered shallow enough to allow almost unlimited bottom time, even on a repetitive dive. However, you still have 159 minutes Residual Time on a dive to twenty feet as an "F" Diver.

Two things make this repetitive dive plan successful. First, the depths are moderate, and second, the deepest dive was done first and shallower dives were done as the day progressed. Following these two general rules in repetitive dive planning will give you more flexibility with surface intervals and bottom times.

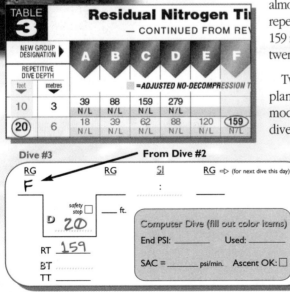

TABLE 3   **Residual Nitrogen Ti**
— CONTINUED FROM REV

NEW GROUP DESIGNATION ▶	A	B	C	D	E	F
REPETITIVE DIVE DEPTH				▥ =ADJUSTED NO-DECOMPRESSION T		
feet ▼ / metres ▼						
10 / 3	39 N/L	88 N/L	159 N/L	279 N/L		
(20) / 6	18 N/L	39 N/L	62 N/L	88 N/L	120 N/L	(159) N/L

Dive #3   **From Dive #2**

RG — F

RG

SI — :

RG ⇨ (for next dive this day)

D 20   safety stop ☐ ___ ft.

RT 159
BT
TT

Computer Dive (fill out color items)
End PSI: _____   Used: _____
SAC = _____ psi/min.   Ascent OK: ☐

Using Computers for Repetitive Diving

As we have described throughout this course, dive computers calculate depth, time and time remaining on a given dive, as well as monitor your ascent rate and warn you if you are ascending too quickly. They also track your surface interval time, and calculate the time you can spend on repetitive dives. Dive computers plan and monitor your data throughout the diving day, and, when used properly, can add many minutes to your dives while remaining within the no-decompression limits.

Common Computer Features

1. **Planning Mode.** This feature allows the user to view no-decompression times for the planned depth and current surface interval time. The user can scroll through various depths and times based on the type of dive he or she wants to do.

2. **Dive Mode.** When the computer enters the water, it automatically switches to dive mode. In dive mode, the computer tracks depth, actual bottom time and remaining no-decompression time for the dive. Most computers report no-decompression information based on altitude, if any previous dives have been done, and what previous surface intervals have been completed. Computers that are air integrated will also report dive time remaining based on the current amount of air in the diver's cylinder, consumption rate and depth.

3. **DiveLog Mode.** Most computers automatically store your dive statistics (depth, actual bottom time, temperature, alarms, altitude, etc.) from the last 5-100 dives you have completed. Use this feature when inputting your dive information into your Total DiveLog System.

4. **Time to Fly.** Most dive computers include a fly time feature. In this mode, the computer reports how much time the diver must wait after diving before flying on an airplane.

5. **Alarms.** Many computers include audible and visual alarms. These alarms can be user adjusted to go off when: a maximum depth has been reached; the user is ascending too fast; the user is close to reaching the no-decompression time limit or the battery is low. In addition, air integrated computers include an alarm option for when the user is low on air.

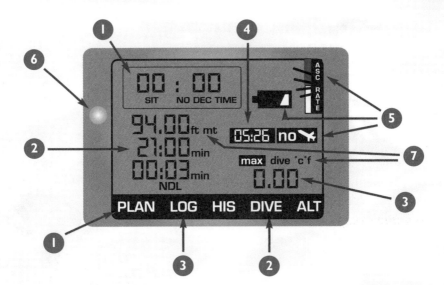

6. **Display Lighting.** Many computers include a user activated display back light for night and low visibility diving.

7. **Units.** The user can set the computer to report information in Imperial or Metric units (on most models).

8. **Personal Computer Integration.** Many dive computers can be connected to a personal computer to download and store dive data. The data can be accessed at any time to analyze dives, consumption rates (for air integrated models) and dive profiles.

9. **Advanced Features.** There are many computers available for various types of diving. If you plan on taking an SSI Nitrox course, you may want to consider a nitrox programmable computer. Likewise, if you will be diving waters that require navigation, you may want to consider a computer with an integrated compass.

Consult your SSI Instructor for more information about computers. He or she can help you determine which computer is best for you based on the type of diving you will be doing and any advanced features you require.

Use Care

It is important to remember that no tools, dive tables or dive computers can guarantee that you will not suffer decompression sickness. Follow the manufacturer's recommendations for their brand and model of computer.

Other Factors Affecting Nitrogen Absorption and Decompression

There are many things that can interfere with the efficient entrance and exit of nitrogen, including:

- Age
- Alcohol or drug use
- Extreme heat or cold
- Old injuries
- Proneness to blood clotting

- Obesity
- Medication
- Loss of sleep
- Extreme fatigue
- Dehydration

Consult with your physician before diving.

1000 feet (305 metres) _____

Sea Level _____

Altitude also affects decompression. When diving at altitude (1000 feet/305 metres above sea level), your nitrogen absorption rate is different than at sea level because of the lower atmospheric pressure, and because diving at altitude is generally done in fresh water.

The U.S. Navy tables were designed for use at sea level and special dive tables have been developed for use in altitude diving. You should be aware that they are based on theoretical models and that there is no standard high altitude table.

Dive computers and depth gauges typically require time to adjust to altitude before they work accurately. When diving at altitude, the higher you go the more conservative you should be.

Flying After Diving

Flying after diving can be harmful for a diver saturated with nitrogen because airplane cabins are not pressurized to sea level pressure.

To avoid problems, it is recommended that you wait 18 hours before flying in a pressurized airplane and 24 hours if you plan to fly, or even drive, above 8000 feet (2.4 kilometres) in a nonpressurized aircraft or vehicle.

SSI Calcuslate

The SSI Calcuslate was designed to help you simplify Surface Consumption Rate (SCR) problems when dive planning. Talk to your SSI Dealer or Instructor about the SSI Calcuslate and how it works.

Divers who have been repetitive diving for several consecutive days should also make an extended surface interval longer than 12 hours and may want to consider taking a day off in the middle of their diving week. Use this extra time for sightseeing or shopping. As an extra measure, it is a good idea to wait 24 hours before flying regardless of other considerations.

Advanced Dive Planning

The SSI Advanced Dive Planning specialty includes more in-depth information on planning your dive, gas consumption and calculating dive times based on various dive parameters and equipment configurations. Ask your SSI Dealer or Instructor for more information about the SSI Advanced Dive Planning Specialty.

Executing Your Dive

Predive Briefing and Buddy Team Functioning

Diving is a shared experience, and it is only enjoyable to the degree that it can be shared. Imagine your excitement upon seeing a gentle giant such as a manta ray for the first time, then turning to show it to someone else, but no one is there. Imagine diving a Spanish warship of the 17th century and finding a 400-year-old cannon, then having no one to tell after you surface.

On the surface, buddies provide the kind of necessary assistance that just makes things go so much easier, such as helping with equipment assembly and with putting on and taking off equipment. You also check the proper positioning and working order of equipment, and your buddy does the same for you. Under water, buddies work together as a team. For example, one buddy can be the leader, in charge of the compass and direction control, while the other buddy monitors depth. A buddy helps in all phases of diving and shares the fun. Always dive with a buddy. He or she provides a second Total Diving System, psychological support and is there to offer help not only underwater, but on the surface when you need an extra hand.

The Buddy System

One of the most important ingredients in enjoyable and responsible diving is the buddy system. You may not think of this as essential to knowing how to dive, or what to do in order to avoid problems while diving, but it is essential to why we dive.

DIVER DIAMOND
SSI
KNOWLEDGE • SKILLS • EQUIPMENT • EXPERIENCE

Another reason for always diving with a buddy is that, naturally, it is safer. In case of a problem, you may need someone there to assist you. Conversely, you are needed as a possible helpmate for your buddy. You make a difference to your buddy; you make his or her dive more comfortable just by being there.

Having a buddy and being a buddy are closely related to another major objective of any dive; being prepared and, consequently, avoiding stress.

If you both know what you are doing, if you have planned your dive and you are following the plan, and if you are both ready to deal with something unexpected, you will have assured yourselves of a comfortable dive.

Solo Diving

The term Solo Diving refers to a type of diving in which a single diver plans and executes a dive without a buddy. When solo diving, additional, redundant equipment is added to offset the increased risk in the event of primary equipment failure. The solo diver must be in outstanding physical condition, and have the correct mental and emotional attitude in order to maintain the level of control required in any emergency situation in which there is no help available.

Diving Alone

Adding additional equipment to the Total Diving System and being in the best physical and mental condition possible cannot entirely compensate for the increased risk associated with diving alone. As mentioned before, the best way to dive is with a buddy.

Predive Briefing

When diving from a charter boat or with any organized group, your diving leader will most likely give a predive briefing about the dive site. The briefing may include specifics such as your dive parameters: how long you can stay down, what direction you can swim, how much air to return with in your cylinder, etc. If the dive is preplanned such as this, you will not need to put as much time into your plan.

When signing up for charters and group dives you may want to find out whether you will be required to follow preplanned dives and stay with the group.

Either way, the following planning information, which is based on the SSI DiveLog page, should be addressed by you and your buddy before diving.

1. **Objective of the Dive.** When making your own dive plan, first talk about why you are diving, and make sure you are both in agreement about your objective. Are you going just to explore coral reefs? Do you plan to investigate a wreck site? Communicate about these things beforehand, and do not suddenly "spring" a new idea on your buddy after your dive has begun; that would not be fair to a buddy who may feel apprehensive about doing something that only you find challenging.

Pressuring an unprepared diver is a sure way of causing stress that can lead to an accident.

2. **Conditions of the Dive.** Your SSI DiveLog provides a convenient check list for site conditions. The type of water, weather and water movement, such as surf and current, may affect different aspects of your dive, such as entries and exits, the amount of thermal protection to wear, how much air you consume and your direction and ability to navigate.

3. **Equipment.** Go over the convenient Equipment Check list in your SSI DiveLog when planning your dive. Knowing what type of suit you wore, cylinder size, special equipment and amount of weight may come in handy when planning future dives, plus it provides a predive checklist to make sure your equipment is ready for diving.

Boat Diving

When boat diving, plan your dive and your equipment assembly, donning, and adjustment such that you are ready to enter the water when the boat reaches the dive site. On chartered trips most decisions may be made for you, but it is certainly smart to check with the captain or dive leader to determine when to get dressed and don equipment.

If you are unfamiliar with your buddy, or if you and your buddy have not been diving in a while, you may want to discuss the following Buddy Check Procedures. These procedures cover some of the differences you may have in your diving skills, emergency training and type of equipment.

4. **Communication.** Effective communication is essential. Both team members must be able to communicate underwater. It is the responsibility of both team members to discuss and agree upon the hand signals that will be used during the dive before the dive begins. Coordinate the hand signals you will use with your buddy, and discuss any other forms of communication you might use during the dive, or on the surface, in an emergency.

"Go up/Going Up"

5. **Lost Buddy Procedure.** Discuss a lost or separated buddy procedure. Discuss how long you will look for your buddy should you become separated and when you will surface for help. One recommended procedure is to make two or three 360° turns in the water, looking for bubbles or other signs of your buddy. If other divers are near, you can signal them to find out if they have seen your buddy. If he/she is nowhere to be found, it is best to surface normally. If your buddy has not surfaced, get help immediately. One reason to dive with a charter or group is the fact that there are other support personnel to assist in an emergency.

6. **Emergency Skills Training.** Discuss how each of you was trained in emergency skills such as air sharing ascents and emergency ascents, because the time to find out is not under water in an emergency. If you discuss your training ahead of time you can be better prepared to handle an emergency.

Dive Profile

The dive profile in your SSI DiveLog will help you record your parameters and plan a repetitive dive.

7. **Equipment Familiarization.** Familiarize yourselves with each other's equipment. What type of power inflator does your buddy have and how does it work? Where is your buddy's alternate air source located and how does it work? What type of configuration is his or her weight system, and how does it detach?

8. **Entry and Exit Procedures.** If you're diving from a boat, you will be informed of the entry and exit procedures. However, if you are diving by yourselves, you and your buddy should discuss the best and easiest methods. Ask the local SSI Dealer if you are unfamiliar with the procedures for the diving conditions at the location.

9. **No-Decompression Dive Plan and Dive Parameters.** Your next step is to plan a no-decompression dive using your computer or the Doppler limits on the U.S. Navy Dive Tables as discussed earlier in this section. Plan your maximum depth and time and have a contingency plan. Plus, you may want to pre-plan your surface interval and what you'll do during that time. You should also discuss your minimum cylinder pressure before resurfacing (it is recommended that you be on the surface with no less than 500 psi/35 bar). Again, some of these decisions may be made for you when diving with a charter or group.

10. Go/No-Go Diving Decision. Last, confirm that both you and your buddy are feeling okay and are still ready to make the dive.

Each diver has the right at any time, for any reason, to call off a dive, even if you are dressed and ready to enter the water.

Your dive buddy might be your spouse or a friend. Your buddy might even be someone who is assigned to you on a boat by the dive leader.

SSI SCUBA SCHOOLS INTERNATIONAL **DiveLog**   DIVE NUMBER _____

Date _____ Buddy _____
Site Name _____
Site Location _____
DIVE OBJECTIVE: ☐ Course: _____   ☐ Fun: _____

EQUIPMENT

EXPOSURE SUIT: ☐ Dive Skin ☐ Wetsuit ☐ Drysuit ☐ Hood
CYLINDER SIZE: _____   ☐ Steel ☐ Aluminum
ACCESSORY EQUIPMENT:
☐ Compass ☐ Light   ☐ Dive Tool ☐ Surface Marker
☐ Camera   Next Time Take: _____
WEIGHT: Amount: _____   ☐ OK* Next Time Try: _____
*If weight is ok, record it on the Proper Weighting Table in the Equipment Record Section

BUDDY CHECK

☐ Hand Signals   ☐ Alt. Air Source Location/Use
☐ Lost Buddy   ☐ Weight System Location/Use
☐ Emergency Procedures   ☐ _____
☐ Power Inflator Location/Use   ☐ Entry & exit procedures

CONDITIONS

TYPE OF DIVE: ☐ Beach/Shore ☐ Boat ☐ Other: _____
WATER: ☐ Salt ☐ Fresh Temperature: _____ Visibility: _____
SURFACE: ☐ Calm ☐ Choppy ☐ Rough
SURF: ☐ Small ☐ Medium ☐ Large **TIDE:** ☐ High ☐ Low ☐ N/A
CURRENT: ☐ Fast ☐ Slow ☐ None Type: _____
WEATHER: ☐ Sunny ☐ Cloudy Temperature: _____

PRE-DIVE

Plan Depth: _____ SAC Rate: _____ Plan Time: _____
Contingency Depth: _____ Contingency Time: _____
Start PSI: _____ psi/min ☐ Air
☐ EAN: _____ % MOD: _____ PO₂: _____
Planned Navigation: ☐ Compass: _____ (Heading) ☐ Natural

PRE-DIVE: Fill this out before you dive

POST DIVE

RG _____ RG _____ SI _____ RG ⇨ (for next dive this day)

safety stop ☐ _____ ft.
D
RT _____
BT _____
TT _____

Computer Dive (fill out color items)
End PSI: _____ Used: _____
SAC = _____ psi/min. Ascent OK: ☐

Buddy Signature _____   # _____
Dive Leader Signature _____   # _____

© Copyright Concept Systems, Inc. 1977
ADRO/SSI ACCESSORIES DIVELOGS OWD LEVEL 1 "Log Page LVL 1-5/02" Art# #1100-H

© Copyright Concept Systems, Inc. 1977
ADRO/SSI ACCESSORIES DIVELOGS OWD LEVEL 1 "Log Page LVL 1-5/02" Art# #1100-H

Revised 1986, 1989, 1990, 1992, 1995, 2002

Avoiding Panic Situations

Avoiding panic situations when diving is a matter of understanding the causes of panic. Listed below are some of the most common causes of panic.

♦ **Breathing Distress.** There are two general causes of breathing distress: actually being low or out of air or the feeling of not getting enough air created by ineffective breathing patterns.

To avoid being low on air or out of air, simply monitor your air supply and plan your dive to return to the surface with at least 500psi (34 bar) of air in your cylinder. To understand and manage ineffective breathing patterns, refer to the information in Section 3 on *Breath Control: Stress Control* and carbon dioxide buildup.

Your Safety First

Whoever your buddy might be, or end up being, always remember that your safety in the open water is the most important factor of any dive and you always have the right to decline diving with someone with whom you do not feel comfortable.

KNOWLEDGE · SKILLS · EQUIPMENT · EXPERIENCE

DIVER DIAMOND
SSI
SCUBA SCHOOLS INTERNATIONAL

♦ **Mistaking Fiction for Reality.** The movie and entertainment industries create fiction from fact for the sake of a great story—a sense of danger, excitement, suspense and adventure. Marine animals, especially sharks, are a popular subject for misrepresentation and the creation of unrealistic fear. Almost all sharks, with a few exceptions are more afraid of us than we are of them. In fact, it is a rare occasion that a diver sees a shark; however, if you do, observe its beauty and treat it with respect. Above all, never assume what a shark will do, they are quite unpredictable.

♦ **Environmental Conditions.** Water movement, limited visibility, underwater drop-offs, entanglement, hazardous marine life, cold, claustrophobia and separation from your buddy may all be related changes in the environment. Analyzing and discussing these issues with your dive leader and buddy during your pre-dive briefing will reduce the possibility of them becoming a problem.

◆ **Equipment.** Using equipment that is unfamiliar, does not fit well or performs inadequately can create stress leading to panic. That is why we recommend selecting and owning as much of your own equipment as possible, and keeping it well maintained by your SSI Dealer. Use your predive checklist and check each piece of equipment before every dive.

◆ **Comfort and Ability.** Diving should always be fun. To help ensure that you do have fun, always dive within your ability and comfort level. Diving outside of your ability level can lead to stress, which leads to panic. Enjoy your dive by staying within your limits, and remember, only you decide when and how you want to dive.

Identifying the Panic Response

Identifying panic and fear in a diver is covered indepth in the SSI Diver Stress and Rescue Specialty course offered by your SSI Dealer; however, it is important for all divers to know the basic signs and symptoms of the panic response.

Here are some ways to identify panic responses in divers:

◆ Erratic, uncoordinated movements,

◆ Wide-eyed fearful look,

◆ Erratic breathing pattern, bubbles seemingly exploding from second stage mouthpiece,

◆ Vertically oriented in the water, kicks ineffective,

◆ Flailing arms, trying to "climb" out of the water and

◆ Difficulty obtaining positive buoyancy on the surface.

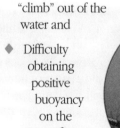

If you observe signs of panic in your buddy while at depth:

◆ Locate your alternate air source in case it is needed,

◆ Approach your buddy and look for the source of the problem,

◆ Face your buddy and get his or her attention. In many cases, the knowledge that you are there is enough for the panicked diver to regain control and

◆ If your buddy's behavior is so erratic that it threatens your safety, back off until he or she calms down. You are not trained to help a diver in an advanced panic stage. Do all you can without endangering yourself.

If you observe signs of panic in your buddy while on the surface:

◆ Completely fill your BC,

◆ Calmly talk to your buddy,

◆ Instruct your buddy to establish positive buoyancy. If required, assist your buddy ditch his or her weights, and fill the BC,

◆ Help your buddy find the position in which breathing is the most comfortable and

◆ Get help if required; do not endanger yourself.

Prevention of Panic

You can avoid panic situations simply by preparing for them.

◆ Obtain proper training in an SSI Open Water Diver Certification Course,

◆ Dive with a high quality Total Diving System and maintain it through your SSI Dealer,

◆ Follow proper diving procedures,

◆ Always dive with a responsible buddy,

◆ Develop confidence by gaining experience through diving and increasing your diving education through SSI Continuing Education and

◆ Do not dive outside of your ability and comfort zones; evaluate your skill and ability honestly and accurately.

Taking Care of Yourself

As we have discussed throughout this program, your diving and travel will be much more enjoyable if you take care of yourself. Here are some of the things you can do to make your diving more enjoyable:

◆ Make sure you consume adequate, nonalcoholic, liquids to prevent dehydration when diving,

◆ Start your diving day with a good breakfast. Light, non-gaseous foods are best,

◆ Eat sensibly throughout the day,

◆ Wear the proper Exposure System for the entire diving day to prevent over and under heating. Remember, the water will "feel" warmer at the start of your day and cooler as the day progresses and your body looses heat and

◆ Refrain from smoking, drinking alcohol or using drugs.

Your Well Being

Your physical and emotional well-being are very important components of fun and comfortable diving, yet they are often overlooked.

DIVER DIAMOND
KNOWLEDGE • SKILLS
EQUIPMENT • EXPERIENCE
SSI

Executing Your Dive: Review

Up to this point, we have discussed proper diving procedures and skills. Although we will not review the entire procedure again, we have created this handy summary which reviews dive procedures.

1. Plan the dive.
2. Assemble and adjust your equipment.
3. Complete a final preentry buddy check.
4. Confirm water conditions and your direction.

5. Make the best and easiest entry for the conditions and platform you are entering from.
6. Follow proper descent procedures, using a line if possible and equalize pressure.
7. Perform your buddy responsibilities, including staying with your buddy (or the group) throughout the dive.

8. Monitor your Information System, and stick to the predetermined dive plan.

9. Breathe normally all the time. Never hold your breath.

10. Maintain neutral buoyancy throughout the dive to conserve energy and avoid damage to the fragile environment.

11. Ascend at the same rate as your buddy, and no faster than 30 feet per minute (9 metres per minute).

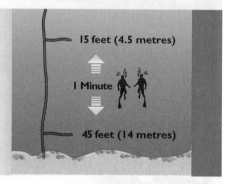

15 feet (4.5 metres)

1 Minute

45 feet (14 metres)

12. Make a safety stop at 15 feet (4.5 metres) for 3 to 5 minutes.

13. Follow proper surface procedures by inflating your BC and keeping your mask and second stage (or snorkel) in place.

14. Make the best and easiest exit for the diving conditions. Stay clear of the boat's dive platform or ladder until it is your turn to exit.

Have fun! After all that is what it is all about.

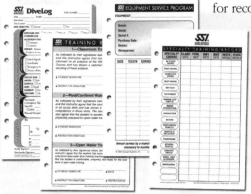

Post Dive Briefing

After you have completed your dive, cleaned your equipment with clean fresh water, and stored it for travel or prepared it for the next dive, you will need to complete a Post Dive Briefing. It is at this time that you will record the dive in your Total DiveLog System using the Total DiveLog Page.

As mentioned in Section 1, there are many practical reasons for logging dives. For one, it helps maintain an accurate dive profile which allows you to plan safe, repetitive dives. In addition, you can record valuable information about the dives you make, such as the dive location, directions, weather and water conditions.

Keeping a history of your air consumption rates will track your comfort level because lower rates indicate greater comfort. It is also a good idea to keep track of the amount of weight you use to achieve neutral buoyancy. You may also want to make notations on what kinds of equipment you used, and what you should purchase before your next dive.

Weight

By keeping track of weight needs in different circumstances, you will be able to know in advance how much weight you will require for a particular dive.

You are probably beginning to see that the SSI Total DiveLog is a handy tool with many purposes. In addition to tracking your number of logged dives, your SSI DiveLog is an important source of information for subsequent dives, for keeping track of your training, and for recording memories. The Total DiveLog is also a record-keeping system for SSI Specialty Courses and Scuba Skills Update programs. The Equipment section helps you record purchases, maintenance, your weighting needs for proper buoyancy and serves as a pre-trip checklist.

Summary

By now in your training as an Open Water Diver you have received the fundamentals. You might say, as the Diver Diamond illustrates, that correct knowledge, proficient skills, proper equipment and diving experience equal enjoyable scuba diving. In this section you learned about a part of diving in which equipment, knowledge and safe skills are inseparable: the U.S. Navy Dive Tables or dive computer and their use in dive planning, and putting all of the information together to execute a dive with your buddy. The rest is up to you. Work with your SSI Instructor, ask questions, and have fun learning and gaining the experience required to become a comfortable, confident diver. Where do we go from here? Now that you know what to do and how to do it, let's take our attention off of you and look at where you will be practicing this newfound excitement called open water diving —Your World Under Water.

KNOWLEDGE · SKILLS · EQUIPMENT · EXPERIENCE

DIVER DIAMOND

SSI
SCUBA SCHOOLS
INTERNATIONAL

Experience

Like all other scuba skills and knowledge, gaining experience using the tables or computer, planning your dives and executing your dive according to plan really is not very hard to do, and it will undoubtedly make you more comfortable as a diver and therefore make diving more enjoyable for you.

Section 4 Study Guide Questions

1. _____ _____ and the _____ _____
   are designed to allow you to make as many repetitive dives per day as
   you would like, as long as you remain within the
   _____ limits.

2. The amount of elapsed time from the start of your descent to the time
   you begin your direct ascent to the surface is called the
   _____ _____ .

3. The deepest point you reached during a dive, no matter how briefly
   you stayed there is called _____ .

4. The letter assigned after a dive which indicates the amount of residual
   nitrogen remaining in the diver's tissues is called the _____
   _____ _____ .

5. Any dive started more than _____ minutes and less than _____
   hours after a previous scuba dive is called a repetitive dive.

6. Residual Time (RT) is defined as _____ nitrogen pressure
   still residual in the diver at the _____ of a repetitive dive.

7. The Surface Interval (SI) is defined as the amount of time the diver
   stays out of the _____ or on the surface _____ dives.

8. Suppose you make a dive to 51 feet (15.5 metres) for 31 minutes. What
   is your group designation? _____ After a surface interval of one
   hour, what is your new group designation? _____

9. Using your new group designation from question 8, suppose you want
   to make a second dive to a depth of 40 feet (12 metres). What is your
   adjusted no-decompression time limit? _____ minutes. What is your
   Residual Time (RT)? _____ minutes.

10. Dive computers plan and monitor your data throughout the _____ _____, and, when used properly, can add many _____ to your dives while remaining within the no-decompression limits.

11. It is important to remember that no tools, dive tables or dive computers can guarantee that you will not suffer _____ _____.

12. When diving at _____, your nitrogen absorption rate is different than at _____ _____ because of the lower atmospheric pressure, and because diving at altitude is generally done in fresh water.

13. To avoid problems it is recommended that you wait _____ hours before flying in a pressurized airplane, and _____ hours if you plan to fly, or even drive, above 8000 feet (2.4 km) in a nonpressurized aircraft of vehicle.

14. Adding additional equipment to the Total Diving System and being in the best physical and mental condition possible _____ entirely compensate for the _____ _____ associated with diving alone.

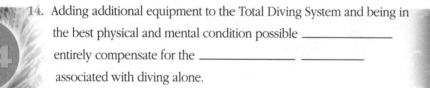

15. Pressuring an _____ diver is a sure way of causing stress that can lead to an accident.

16. The _____ _____ in your SSI DiveLog will help you record your parameters and plan a repetitive dive.

17. Each diver has the right at any time, for any reason, to _____ _____ a _____, even if you are dressed and ready to enter the water.

18. Diving should always be fun. To help ensure that you do have fun, always dive within your _____ and _____ level.

19. Some things you can do to make your diving more enjoyable include drinking adequate, _____ liquids to prevent dehydration and eating _____ throughout the day.

20. In addition to tracking number of logged dives, your _____ _____ is an important source of information for subsequent dives, for keeping track of your training, and for recording _____.

Your Underwater World

This adventure will begin with some necessary emphasis on the formation and makeup of water environments which harbor fascinating plants and animals.

5

One thing we cannot escape — forever afterward, throughout all our life, the memory of the magic of water and its life, of the home which was once our own — this will never leave us.

— **William Beebe**

SCUBA SCHOOLS
INTERNATIONAL

Scuba divers have the unique privilege of enjoying the beauty of the underwater world. Scuba Schools International believes that the more you know about the aquatic world, the better diver you will be and the more you will respect and appreciate its value. This section includes basic knowledge and practical information about diving in the ocean, followed by an introduction to underwater life.

In the early days of sport diving, the ocean was seen by many as an indestructible, self-renewing resource. We know now that it can be fragile at the hands of human technology and exploration. We also know that it has an impressive capacity for regeneration when given the chance.

Always dive as a visitor, as the guest that you are, in this new environment. As long as you do, you will be welcomed and have many opportunities to return.

Section 5 Objectives
After completing this section you will

◆ Understand the fundamentals of wave, tide and current action,

◆ Be able to explain how wave, tide and current action affect divers,

◆ Understand what surge and surf are.

◆ Understand proper diving techniques as they relate to surge and surf,

◆ Be able to explain how coral reefs form and their global importance and

◆ Be able to identify many species of marine life including potentially hazardous marine life.

Scuba Schools International supports the ongoing efforts of the diving industry to protect our oceans, coral reefs and all aquatic environments for future generations. As an SSI diver, we encourage and invite you to share responsibility for protecting these valuable resources. One simple way you can participate is to embrace a personal ethic of leaving the natural world the way you find it. Many dive boats and dive resorts already have this policy; you can model and support it.

Your behavior can help ensure that divers of the future will still be able to experience and enjoy the beauty of innerspace.

The Ocean Environment

The ocean contains a multitude of organisms, but at the same time it can be thought of as an organism itself. Though there is no way to know exactly what happened, we can speculate on the "birth" of the oceans and their evolution. Later in this chapter we will look at various inhabitants of the ocean, but for now let's discuss the ocean itself, how it developed, how it lives and breathes and how we are connected to it.

How Much Water?

The surface of this planet is actually made up of very little earth. It is, in fact, about 72% water.

DIVER DIAMOND
SSI
KNOWLEDGE • SKILLS • EQUIPMENT • EXPERIENCE

We only call the globe upon which we walk "Earth" because we are land inhabitants, and as the inventors of language, it is our self-assigned privilege to call it whatever we want. If a whale, on the other hand, was capable of having "ideas" in our sense of the word, its idea of a name for this place would no doubt be different.

Theories on how the oceans formed vary, but it is generally agreed that they are the product of condensing vapors which were left in the aftermath of the cosmic fireworks which began the formation of Earth and the volcanic activity which continued for ages during the early history of Earth. As the Earth cooled, these vapors condensed and fell as torrential rain, collecting in the low

Sea Water

Even though sea water tastes very salty, the salinity is actually only about 3.5%. But this salinity is made up of a high concentration of nutrients, which forms the basic food for the multitude of plants and animals that inhabit the seas.

DIVER DIAMOND
SSI
KNOWLEDGE • SKILLS • EQUIPMENT • EXPERIENCE

spots of this young planet. These rains continued until the oceans contained their current volume of nearly 1.5 billion cubic kilometres of water — a lot of water!

As these rains fell they washed minerals into the depths. Also, volcanic activity continued under water as well as on land, and what we now know as the oceans became receptacles for huge amounts of minerals. This resulted in the high degree of salinity that is characteristic of the oceans' salt water.

The ocean remains today an extremely important source of life in that it is the home for many of the first links in the earth's food chain. Photosynthesis in plants creates oxygen in the oceans just as it does on land, and this initiates the process of creating organic nutrients which serve to feed more complex organisms, which in turn are fed upon by larger organisms, and so on. Animal waste and plant and animal decomposition complete the food cycle by replenishing the sea's basic nutrients and starting the chain of life all over again.

It is estimated that the plant production in the oceans may be ten times more than that on land. More than 85% of the oxygen is produced by marine plants. Even the photosynthesis that takes place on land requires water, which originates in the oceans.

In fact, inland waters are merely products of ocean water which have evaporated and condensed and have then fallen as rain or melted from snowcaps and glaciers. Why, then, do inland waters lack the salt content of the oceans? There are a couple reasons for this. First, water, as it evaporates, leaves minerals behind; when salt water evaporates, most of the salt stays in the ocean and fresh water is held by air until it falls as rain or snow. Second, any remaining salinity is removed by the process of freezing, which takes place in the polar and mountainous regions. As this ice melts, freshwater rivers and lakes are formed. Larger inland freshwater areas, such as the Great Lakes of the United States, were formed over many thousands of years of warming temperatures, which gradually melted glaciers. Ultimately, all of this fresh water flows back into the oceans to complete the cycle of water.

The Great Lakes

We are all linked directly or indirectly to the ocean. The ocean is the world's great caretaker. We all need to do our part to keep the oceans clean and free of pollutants; we must leave her in a pristine state if we expect to go on enjoying her natural beauty.

For us as divers, the oceans may be playgrounds, but playgrounds are only fun and exciting if we keep them clean and well maintained.

Water Movement and Diving

So vast is the amount of water on Earth, we have only recently begun to gain an understanding of such things as its life cycles, as mentioned above, and other phenomena, such as the mechanics of water movement — basically how water "acts" when subject to particular conditions. Tides and currents, waves and surf all have some effect on divers and need to be understood in order to make dive planning more efficient and safe.

Tides

The tide is an example of a wave, but it is the largest example on Earth and the most dynamic water movement worldwide. Its wavelength, in fact, is half the circumference of the earth. The force that originally acts on the water to create tide is the gravity of the moon and sun, primarily the moon, pulling at the side of the earth nearest the moon.

Low tide: where the bulge of water is the shallowest.

Water is spun away from Earth by centrifugal force.

Water is pulled away from Earth by the gravitational force of the moon and the sun.

High tide: where the bulge of water is the deepest.

The centrifugal force of the earth's rotation pulls at the water in the opposite direction from the moon's pull. What results is a fairly steady-state "bulge" of water on the earth's surface. This gravitational/centrifugal force has a rubber band effect in that the water on the opposite side of the earth bulges in proportion to the gravity side.

The bulge seems to roll across the surface as the earth rotates and the moon orbits. But, as you will soon learn about waves, it is not the water that moves forward, it is the wave-creating energy that moves forward; similarly, it is the bulge of tide that moves forward, not the water in the bulge.

When this bulge approaches a coastline, the water level rises and engulfs a greater portion of the shoreline than before. This vertical increase in water level is called high tide. At the same time the bulge is located at one area of the globe, the water, which is pulled away and into the bulge leaves behind areas of low tide. Naturally, when this drop in water level occurs on a coastline, more of the shore is exposed. When the tide changes direction there is a period of no vertical movement in water level, and this is called the stand.

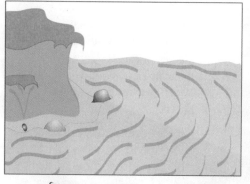

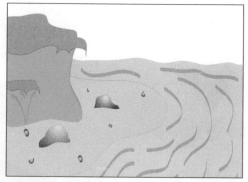

High tide

Low tide

Tides will enter into your dive planning. Near shore, the best time for diving would probably be during periods of minimal exchange of water between the tides. However, if you are going to make a very shallow dive on the open coast, the best time to go is at the peak of high tide to give greater depth and to reduce surge.

One instance when you may want to enter during low tide is if you are snorkeling; low tide will maximize your effective time under water. The extent of tidal interchange may also have a considerable effect on the visibility.

Tidal Currents

The water which constitutes the tidal bulge is lifted, but does not move forward. However, as the tide moves across the face of the earth it creates a kind of "wake" which follows. This is called a tidal current. As tide comes to shore, a flood current follows.

Tidal currents are of more interest to divers than the tides themselves. The currents cause water movement toward and away from shore, which can affect divers' entries and exits and can cause resistance for a diver swimming in the opposite direction of the current. This

More Tides

As the tide moves outward from shore, an ebb current follows. The period between the currents when no movement occurs is called slack time. Though the tidal currents and the slack time are related to the tides and the stand, they do not occur at the same time.

DIVER
DIAMOND
SSI
KNOWLEDGE SKILLS EQUIPMENT EXPERIENCE

High Tide

Low Tide

is especially critical in mouths of bays and lagoons. Tidal currents can also combine with other, more localized water movements, causing conflict which may result in unsteady waters.

It is, of course, always a good idea to dive in waters as calm as possible, and concerning tidal currents, this would ideally be during slack time. In many parts of the ocean, tidal currents will not figure into dive planning as much as more localized water movements such as waves and surf.

Ocean Currents

Another example of water movement on a global and/or local scale is ocean currents. These are caused by the sun heating different areas of the earth with varying intensity, combined with the effect of the rotation of the earth, resulting in different water temperatures. The water nearer the equator is warmer.

At the surface there are permanent ocean-wide currents, or "streams." The six major streams are located such that there is one in each hemisphere of the Pacific, Atlantic and Indian Oceans. These currents transplant warmer waters northward or colder waters southward along the coasts. This explains the presence of subtropical plants and animals off Florida and southern Japan, while Southern California is bathed by cold temperatures.

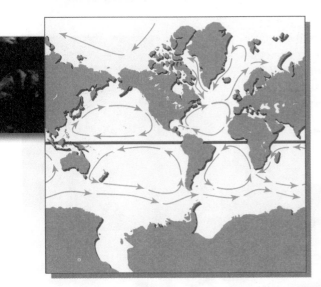

Global Ocean Currents

Thermoclines

Because dense, cold water tends to sink underneath warm water, layers of various temperatures are found at different depths. The boundaries between these layers are called thermoclines. There are areas of sharply changing temperatures within a relatively narrow depth range. This occurs in all water bodies, and in the oceans, thermoclines form at depths which often concern the sport diver, especially while diving in nontropical waters. Below the top 600 feet (183 metres) or so the temperature stays about the same much of the year, but at various layers above this depth, temperatures may fluctuate considerably, and divers must, therefore, incorporate local temperatures into their dive planning.

Waters in the shallowest depths may change by 4 to 5 degrees overnight in some areas.

Also of concern to sport divers are the periods of colder waters cycling downward. During the winter and summer months oceans and temperate lakes usually remain stratified with a fairly stable thermocline at some depth, but during spring and fall the seasonal change results in sudden drops or increases in temperatures at the surface. This surface water cools or heats, becoming more or less dense, and the colder water sinks to seek a level of water with the same temperature. Wind can also cause a mixing of water resulting in deeper water becoming warmer. This cycling of water is called overturn. While these changes are taking place, divers can actually feel temperature differences just by moving slightly to one side or another, or by ascending or descending a few feet.

In fresh waters the diver is very likely to experience sharp temperature differences from one temperature layer to the next, even when stratified, merely because of the small sizes and shallower depths of lakes as compared to oceans.

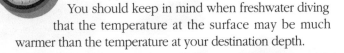

You should keep in mind when freshwater diving that the temperature at the surface may be much warmer than the temperature at your destination depth.

Use the proper exposure system according to the temperature you will encounter at the destination depth, not according to what is adequate at the surface. The same applies for most nontropical ocean diving, and to a much more limited extent, to tropical diving.

Waves

Cold polar air acts the same way cold polar water does. It descends, travels toward the equator, then warms and rises, creating several cyclical flows worldwide. When this air movement is near the earth's surface we call it wind; when wind comes into contact with water, water movement of particular interest to divers — waves, surge and surf — is formed at the surface.

Waves are generated in one of two ways: by wind or by seismic activity on or near the ocean floor. By far the most common cause of waves is wind.

All wind waves are formed the same way. To imagine how waves are formed, first imagine a smooth water surface. As the wind comes into contact with the water, the friction of that contact lifts up small ripples in the water. The ripples slope upward and create a larger area against which the wind continues to blow. This increases the area of resistance that the wind can act upon, and larger and larger wavelets and waves are formed.

Three things determine how big the waves will get:

♦ How hard the wind blows (velocity),

♦ How long the wind continues to blow (time) and

♦ Over what distance the wind continues to blow unimpeded (the fetch).

Wave Action

The longer and harder the wind blows, the larger the waves become. The longer the fetch, the further the wave action will be extended.

DIVER DIAMOND
SSI
KNOWLEDGE SKILLS EQUIPMENT EXPERIENCE

The three factors mentioned above determine the height of waves, and wave height is related to wavelength. Wavelength is measured from the crest of one wave to the crest of the next wave, with the wave trough lying between. The height of the wave is related to the wavelength at a ratio of about 1:7. That is, if the wavelength is 7 feet (2.1 metres), the height will range around 1 foot (.3 metre). If the wavelength is 21 feet (6 metres), the height will range around 3 feet (1 metre). The period of a wave is the time it takes for a wave to pass a fixed point, and as such is related to wavelength.

Wavelength

Height | Crest

Trough

When a wave reaches a height that sets the water at a considerable angle from the horizontal, it either collapses under its own weight or, in the case of a strong wind, the top is blown off, creating the condition we call whitecaps. In open waters, as larger waves break, smaller ones form in the trough.

Or waves from different directions mix together and eventually a somewhat regular pattern of larger groups of waves followed by smaller groups forms beyond the area of the fetch. This continual pattern is known as sea.

Continual Wave Motion

No matter what the origin of waves, what sets a continual wave action in motion is the energy which results from the building up and collapsing of waves.

Sometimes a relatively stable sea will be disturbed by wave energy coming from conflicting directions, resulting in a sea that essentially moves in two or more different directions. This is known as confused sea, and is often the cause of sea sickness — even affecting the "old salts" at times.

Seismic waves originate differently than wind waves. If there is a geological plate shift or some kind of volcanic disturbance underwater, a sudden rise or collapse in the earth's crust on the ocean floor causes the water above to follow suit. A sudden void results on the water's surface, and it is immediately filled in by surrounding water. This sets up a chain reaction which perpetuates energy, resulting in long period/long wavelength waves. When such waves are predicted to arrive at a coastline site, monstrous waves can result. No diving should take place during this time.

Seismic Wave Formation

In deep water, the water particles in waves at a given site actually move in a circular pattern. They are at the top of the circle in the peak of the wave, and at the bottom of the circle in the trough. Instead of water moving forward, the energy is transferred forward by one wave to the next, and so on. It is the energy which moves forward, not the water in the waves themselves. Think of the action of a length of rope you hold at one end and then whip. A wave travels down the rope, but the rope stays in the same place. What

Wave Energy

travels is energy, not the rope. Electricity moving through a wire demonstrates the same principle.

Wave energy can travel for long distances and result in waves of varying size and strength. The energy only slows and refracts when

something interrupts it. One way this can happen is when wave energy comes into contact with the ocean bottom near the shoreline. This is what causes the water movement we call surge and surf.

We will discuss surge and surf more in depth shortly, as surf can be of significant concern to the diver making shore entries and exits. First we will look at some of the things boat divers need to be concerned with regarding water movement.

Entries and Exits When Boat Diving

For the most part, boat captains will exercise caution in locating an area with relatively calm water. Nevertheless, there are different water conditions in different regions, and those conditions plus the personal preferences of boat captains will dictate what entry and exit techniques you use. Be alert for these during your predive briefing.

Regardless of other factors, when boat diving in the open water there are some general rules to follow in every case. Boats rise and fall with the motion of waves and swells. When entering or exiting a boat using a ladder or dive deck, mount or dismount when the boat dips into a wave trough.

Hold On!

It is important to hold on when entering the boat because while your equipment feels weightless in water, as soon as you emerge from the water, it will weigh you down and you may instantaneously feel the full weight of your body and equipment transferred to your arms. To shift your centre of mass, lean forward slightly and offset this weight.

Keep your equipment on until you are safely on deck. The only exceptions to this include removing fins to climb a ladder, removing your weight belt to make you more positively buoyant, and removing equipment and handing it up if instructed to do so by your boat captain.

Take these precautions in case you accidentally slip back into the water: Keep your mask in place so you can see, your regulator or snorkel in place so you can breathe, and your BC inflated so you can float.

If you would like to learn more about diving from boats, especially in high seas, ask your local SSI Dealer about a Specialty Course in Boat Diving.

Surf and Surge

As described earlier, when waves or swells travel in deep water, the individual water particles are moving in a circle. Only the wave of energy moves forward. This circular movement of the water continues to a depth equal to about half the length of the wave. Remember, length is measured from peak to peak, or trough to trough.

As the wave approaches shore, this circular movement of water begins to contact the bottom. The circular movement gradually flattens out and changes the energy to a back and forth motion called surge. Surge can be a gentle, rhythmic back and forth movement, or it can be a high velocity, undiveable movement. The higher the

Avoiding Seasickness

If you are susceptible to seasickness, ask a diving physician for medication, and also inform your group leader so that you can enter the water as soon as possible when you reach your destination. By confirming your plan, assembling your equipment, and preparing to dress before arriving at your dive site, you can minimize the time spent on deck once the boat is anchored.

wave is, in relation to its length, the greater the energy in the surge. Further, the longer the wavelength, the deeper in depth the surge will be felt.

Each diver will discover how much surge they can dive in comfortably. It is important to remember that surge will almost always diminish as a diver goes deeper.

Surge

Under water divers experience surge, the back and forth movement of water caused by the energy of waves. The bigger the waves, the stronger the surge. To avoid strong surge, move a little deeper.

KNOWLEDGE • SKILLS • EQUIPMENT • EXPERIENCE

DIVER DIAMOND

SSI
SCUBA SCHOOLS INTERNATIONAL

When the circular movement of the water particles contact the bottom and create surge, it also slows the movement of the water particles at the bottom, while the water at the top continues unabated. This results in a steepening of the wave. When the steepness of the waves exceeds a certain angle, or the speed of the water particles at the top of the circle exceeds the forward motion of the wave, the tops of the waves collapse and the waves break. At this point the water particles move toward the beach. These breaking waves are what we call surf. The movement of water returning from shore back to the ocean is called the backwash.

Breaking Wave Energy

Since the wave of energy travels toward the beach over fairly even lengths of shoreline in certain places, you will sometimes see a pattern or series of waves parallel to shoreline. When surf is very powerful and steady, this pattern can form a hollow space under the crest resulting in the "tube" or "pipeline" of surfing fame.

5

There are three types of breakers:

When the wave breaks slowly and spills evenly over the top, it is a spilling breaker.

When the water curls over and breaks all at once in a crash, it is a plunging breaker.

When the water peaks up and spouts, it is a surging breaker. Surging breakers happen in areas where there is an abrupt change at shoreline without a gradual approach, such as rocky cliffs or a very steep beach where the waves crash against a nearly vertical shore.

The area between the points at which the largest and smallest waves break is called the surf zone.

Entering and Exiting Surf

When entering or exiting from shore, the diver's primary concern is to avoid being knocked down and buffeted by surf and backwash. Once a diver has fallen down in a surf zone, large quantities of tumbling water can remove pieces of equipment and cause disorientation and serious injury.

Surf conditions vary widely throughout the world, so there is no absolute method for entry or exit that will cover all conditions. The first time that you dive in this type of environment, or any new diving environment, it is recommended that you dive with a local SSI Dealer, Instructor or DiveCon. Also, when entering an unfamiliar area, if there are other divers nearby, watch how they make successful entries and exits. As a general rule, always choose a place with the least water movement.

Wave Patterns

Waves usually enter shore in a pattern: a larger set of waves followed by a smaller set, followed by a larger set, etc. Observe this pattern and time your entries and exits to coincide with a smaller set.

If the surf is large enough to cause loss of balance, you will follow a procedure that will get you into the water safely and past the surf zone quickly. With your mask and fins already on, your regulator in place and your BC inflated, interlock arms with your buddy, hold your mask in place and then shuffle backwards or sideways into the water until you are deep enough to swim. Watch the surf, and when it is about to break, stop and brace yourselves against it, then use the backwash to help move you into waist-deep water. Finally turn and swim out, under or through the waves, not over them. Your objectives are to avoid the concentration of power at the point where water breaks, to get beyond the surf zone and, if possible, to let the backwash help you move outward. (As a safety precaution, this method is recommended for all beach entries, regardless of conditions.)

If the approach to the surf is smooth with gentle slopes, and the surf consists of very gentle, regularly spaced swells, hold your fins and wear all other equipment as you walk into the water until about waist deep. Then, using your buddy for assistance, either cross one leg over the other in a "figure 4" and pull the fins on or lie back in the water with your BC inflated and put them on. Then place the regulator in your mouth and when you and your buddy are ready, swim out through the surf line. (This method should only be done in very calm conditions.)

Exiting surf is often much easier than entering. On an even shore under gentle conditions, just swim near the bottom where water movement is minimal or find a shoreward-moving current to help bring you in. Let the water wash you up to a place where you can stand up and remain stable; remove your fins and walk up.

Follow the same procedures in heavy surf or on an uneven shore. In addition, be sure to keep all your equipment on and the regulator in your mouth. Let the water wash you up until you touch bottom and then crawl to a point where you can safely stand up and remove your fins. Do not turn around and sit down; this is a sure position from which to be knocked down by breaking water.

Exit on an even beach and in an area of gentle surf whenever possible.

When choosing a dive site, stay away from rocky shores and heavy water action. Also avoid choppy offshore waters, which are the result of waves and currents entering shore from different directions at different speeds. This interaction causes turbulence that can reduce visibility and create unusually large waves.

Localized Currents

Localized currents, or currents that run near shorelines, are either one of two types. Longshore currents flow alongside shorelines and are generated by waves which approach a shore at an angle and then are kept from immediately returning oceanward by other incoming waves. When waves hit the shoreline at an angle the water "glances off," but in certain areas it is held back by shoreward moving water. What results is a steady, slow-moving current running parallel to the shoreline.

LONGSHORE CURRENT

Any time waves reach a shoreline, the water must return to the sea. This returning water creates a back current, or rip current. Depending on the size and frequency of waves approaching a shore, the direction from which they contact the shore and the shape of the shoreline results in rip currents of varying directions and strengths.

Submerged Bar

Submerged Bar

RIP CURRENT

This returning water will always follow the path of least resistance. A rip current may be channeled through a low point between two sand bars or it could form a trough in a soft, sandy area near a more solid bottom formation.

ged Bar

RIP CURRENT

Submer

When waves enter a cove or a curved area of a shoreline, the returning water may flow in two different directions forming a rip current. Water reaching a point on the bank, such as, near the north end of the cove, will flow to the south. Water that meets the south bank will flow to the north. When the two flows meet, they will funnel together and form a rip current.

Diving with Localized Currents

When shore diving, you can enter the rip current and allow it to float you out, then plan your exit so that you come back with the shoreward movement of waves. However, if you try to exit at the same point you entered, you will be facing into the rip current. When you use a rip current to carry you out, plan an exit that will allow you to avoid it on your way back.

Locate the Rip Current

It is often possible to see where the rip current is by noticing where there are areas of no waves or lower waves in the surf line. Because the outward moving energy of the rip current cancels out the incoming energy of the waves or surf, you may also be able to see foam on the surface that is moving away from shore.

Any time you do find yourself facing into a rip current, turn and swim at a right angle or diagonal to it until you catch a shoreward water movement, or at least move out of the main force of the current.

If waves approach an even shoreline straight on, rip currents that run opposite the direction of the waves may occur in several different places. If you get caught swimming into a rip current upon your return to shore you can escape it by swimming to one side or another. You will eventually swim around it.

You can predict the strength of a rip current by observing the conditions under which it must travel. If, for instance, it travels through a very narrow channel between submerged bars, it will move with an intense velocity. It would therefore be a good idea to avoid diving in the space between submerged bars.

Swim this direction

RIP CURRENT

An easy way to recognize the location of submerged bars offshore is to notice where surf develops before getting to the shoreline. This indicates wave energy coming into contact with shallow bottom formations offshore.

When boat diving in an area of localized current, you will usually be able to tell the direction of the current by the way the boat anchors. After anchoring, unless affected more by the wind than the current, the boat will tend to swing into the current away from the anchor, stretching the anchor line in the direction of the current as the water pushes at the boat. Watch objects floating beneath the surface of the water to estimate the current's speed. If it is extremely swift, you should move to a different area.

CURRENT

When you make a dive plan keep in mind that you make a safety stop of 3-5 minutes at 15 feet (4.5 metres) on every dive. You need to take this into consideration when boat diving. It is now best to swim against the current during your entire dive (or at least two-thirds of your dive) so that you will still be upstream of the boat when you surface after your safety stop. The best situation is to be able to ascend on the anchor, or ascent , line so that you will be at the boat when you surface.

It is sometimes convenient to descend on an anchor line to get below the current before swimming. Many times a trail line or current line is also used in boat diving. This is a line extended off the stern of the boat for divers to hold onto before and after a dive. This is convenient in areas of current. Divers enter and hold onto the line while waiting for others so that they can all descend and begin the dive together. The trail line is also handy in exiting. It gives divers a stronghold before mounting a ladder or dive deck when located in a current.

Another kind of boat diving allows the diver to move along with a longshore or offshore ocean current. In drift diving you simply float along with the current, along with the boat. When you surface, the boat picks you up.

Always become aware of local water conditions, including the location and intensity of localized currents, before diving. You can consult tidal current tables or ask an SSI Dealer or Instructor located in the particular area where you plan to dive.

Underwater Life

The small portion of this planet on which we humans live is also inhabited by various animals. Because we dominate our environment, many of these other land dwellers have learned to hide from us and avoid contact with us.

One of the most exciting things about exploring under water is that many life forms in water environments have not yet learned to fear us (and hopefully will never have to).

What this means for the diver is that you often will see what you came to see. The sheer amount and variety of life in the oceans and waterways also contributes to the fact that you will surely see some spectacular beauty, create memories and have experiences you will never forget.

Life Under Water

Some aquatic wildlife are larger, such as the barracuda and ray, and some are hardly visible. Others are not so visibly active, such as animals that live inside the coral structures. The greatest variety of life will be visible near the coral reefs in equatorial waters. It is here that the food chain begins. If you are interested in learning more about marine life and, or photographing marine life, talk to your SSI Instructor or Dealer about the SSI Photography and Marine Life Identification Specialty courses.

Marine Parks

Many dive sites throughout the world are considered marine parks and are protected by law. This protection helps keep these dive sites in pristine condition by protecting the coral and other aquatic marine life from hunters and collectors. However, with this protection comes regulation and responsibility. It is up to all divers to respect local laws and to help protect the corals and sea life in these parks.

The Coral Reef

Corals are colonial animals which construct skeletal structures of limestone, often forming extensive reefs in the shallower tropical seas where sunlight and warmer waters prevail. Coral animals, or polyps, attach permanently to a surface such as a rock face, and slowly build around themselves the protective structures and networks we see as the coral reefs. These may form as deep as

250 feet (80 metres), although the majority of the species live at much shallower depths.

As well as simply being beautiful to look at, the reef serves a variety of functions. It offers a home and protection for many species of animals. It is also a source of food for some. As these animals eat the coral, the residue becomes sand. The corals also harbor important algae called zooxanthellae. The algae provide needed oxygen for the coral, and the coral gives off carbon dioxide which the algae in turn need.

Some corals can be brittle, and some are capable of inflicting abrasions or cuts. These corals are also easily damaged by careless divers who kick corals with their fins, or hit the reefs with their cylinders. To avoid injuring yourself or the coral, always maintain neutral buoyancy and practice good buoyancy control over reefs. It is also recommended that you stay a safe distance from the reef to avoid damage. It is best to appreciate the reefs with the eyes rather than the hands. Simply touching the corals may remove some of their protective mucous coating, making them susceptible to injury or infections.

Reef Facts

Most of the healthy coral reefs in existence in the oceans were probably first formed around 200-300 million years ago, and they have persisted throughout the ages because the delicate balance in nature has kept the ocean waters clear and unpolluted.

Of the many varieties of coral, we will only look closely at a few which are most common and that you are most likely to see in warm areas. They fall into two general categories: hard and soft corals. After looking at a few examples of coral, we will cover some of the other varieties of life forms which inhabit the coral reef.

Hard Corals

Among the more eye-pleasing of the hard corals is elkhorn coral. It forms a major portion of the reefs, and it is seen in great quantity, particularly in the Caribbean. It is very sharp, and you can easily cut yourself if you come into contact with it. The staghorn coral grows similar to the elkhorn but is more cylindrical. The brain coral is one of the more intriguing sights in the coral reef. Opening in floral bursts, which

Elkhorn Coral

Staghorn Coral

cling closely to rocks and other hard surfaces, is the star coral. The fire coral is so named because of both its upward plumes of "flame" and because it can inflict a burning sting if you touch the nematocysts. It is not actually a coral, but a hydroid. Keep your distance from fire coral. A hard coral which may give the illusion of being soft is the lettuce leaf.

Star Coral

Fire Coral

Lettuce Leaf

Fire Coral

Soft Corals

The gorgonian corals are soft and flexible. Among the most beautiful soft corals is the sea fan, which takes different forms at different depths. In shallower waters its height ranges from 12 to 24 inches (30 to 60 cm). The deepwater sea fan can get huge, sometimes ten feet (3 metres) across. Black and red coral are other examples of the soft corals.

Sea Fan Corals

Worms

What we normally think of as worms are not what you are likely to see under water. Probably the most conspicuous, and those that are favorites of underwater photographers, are the segmented worms which construct sand or calcareous tubes. These include the feather duster and the Christmas tree worms, sometimes called tube worms. Since these worms live in tubes, the diver normally only views the filter-feeding end of the worm. This end looks like a number of concentric, sometimes brilliantly

Black and Red Coral

Feather Duster

Christmas Tree Worm

colored, or patterned rings. When viewed from the side they look like a miniature evergreens.

Mollusks

The most archaic form of the mollusk is the gastropod. There are more than 35,000 species known, which include snails, abalone and conch. The bivalves, or two-shelled mollusks, include the clam, oyster, mussel and scallop. There are nearly as many species of bivalves as there are gastropods.

Flamingo Tongue

The cephalopods, more commonly known as the squid and octopus, are the largest of all known invertebrates. They are highly developed, having several arms and the ability to move by forcing water out of a deep mantle cavity.

Squid

Octopus

Crustaceans

The group called arthropod includes insects, but also includes a class of animal of more interest to the diver, the crustaceans — lobsters, crabs and shrimp. They are characterized by jointed appendages and external skeletons. Where local regulations allow the harvest of these animals, the diver must be familiar with minimum sizes, numbers allowed, hunting hours and seasons. The diver must respect these local regulations.

Crab

Hermit Crab

Lobster

Echinoderms

Sea stars, brittle stars, sea urchins, sand dollars and sea cucumbers all belong to the group of animals known as the echinoderms. This entire group is marine, with no known fresh water examples. They have a five-

Sea Star

sided radial symmetry with an internal skeleton of small bones. The urchins and cucumbers are prized as a food source in some cultures.

Sea Urchin

Sea Cucumber

Vertebrates

The vertebrates, fishes and mammals, are well known and are the most visible life forms in the open waters. For the interest of the diver we will look at examples divided by environment. If you are particularly interested in sea life, it is recommended that you talk to your SSI Dealer or Instructor or do some reading about local varieties before you go diving.

If you plan on hunting, pay special attention to local regulations governing licensing, limits, gaming seasons and marine parks. Mammals, of course, are fully protected.

Tropical Reef Fish

The reefs are truly amazing in their wealth of life. While the corals themselves are alive, they are inhabited by a vast range of life forms, from microorganisms to large pelagic fish. Most commonly seen are the smaller reef fish which make the caves, crevices and hollows of the reef their home and shelter. An interesting aspect of life in the reef is that its inhabitants are territorial; larger fish will claim and control a portion of the reef with dimensions of several feet, and even the tiniest fish control areas of perhaps only a few inches. The following fish are the most commonly seen when diving at Cozumel, Roatan, Belize, Cayman and the Bahamas.

Lots of Fish!

There is not room in this manual to show you all of this planet's estimated 40,000 species of fish, but in this section you will see some of the species you are most likely to encounter while diving.

Fish Identification

When identifying and describing fish, it is important to understand what the basic parts of the fish are. The diagram below illustrates the basic parts of a fish for identification purposes.

Dorsal Fin

Lateral Line

Tail Fin

Pectoral Fin

Anal Fin

Ventral Fin

Grey Angel

Some of the most common and often seen groups are the varieties of angel fish. They are also some of the most beautiful and, as such, are best appreciated by the eye — they are not considered edible. There are four common types of angel fish. The Grey Angel is distinguished by its spotted grey markings. It is a friendly fish and will occasionally allow a diver to pet it. Another of the angels is the French Angel which is black with bright yellow scales, easily distinguished from its neighbors.

The Blue and Queen Angels are a little harder to tell apart. The Queen is distinguished by the "crown" marking above its head.

French Angel

Queen Angel

Emperor Angel

Blue Angel

The butterfly fish is often confused with the angel. The Puerto Rican Butterfly is also known as the "banded" butterfly. Another variety is the Spotfin. Butterfly fish are quite tame and have no apparent enemies.

Other colorful, but inedible, members of the reef population include the Rock Beauty, the Black Durgeon which is distinguished by bright purple lines at the dorsal and anal fins, the Queen Trigger,

Banded Butterfly

Black Durgeon

Spotfin Butterfly

Rock Beauty

the Glasseye, the phosphorescent purple and yellow Fairy Basslet and the tiny Squirrel Fish.

Other reef dwellers are considered edible. Among the most highly prized

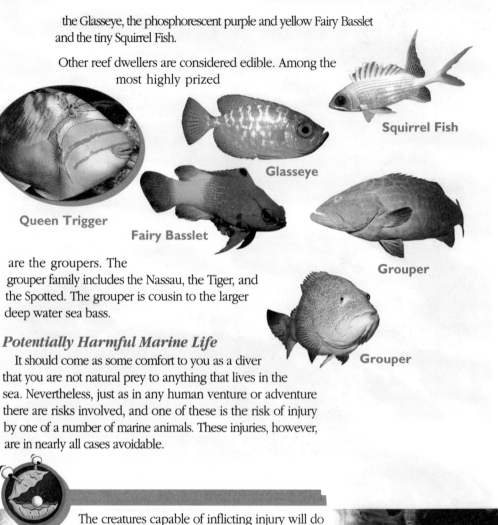

Squirrel Fish

Glasseye

Queen Trigger

Fairy Basslet

Grouper

are the groupers. The grouper family includes the Nassau, the Tiger, and the Spotted. The grouper is cousin to the larger deep water sea bass.

Grouper

Potentially Harmful Marine Life

It should come as some comfort to you as a diver that you are not natural prey to anything that lives in the sea. Nevertheless, just as in any human venture or adventure there are risks involved, and one of these is the risk of injury by one of a number of marine animals. These injuries, however, are in nearly all cases avoidable.

The creatures capable of inflicting injury will do so only defensively. They will react when surprised by being touched or having their territory invaded, or when taunted and molested. Both are defensive reactions.

Being too large to be considered food for any marine animal, humans incur injury as a result of negligence, ignorance and their own aggressive behavior.

By far the most common injuries are ones which occur when an animal is surprised and instinctively protects itself. This happens when a diver accidentally brushes against, grabs or steps on something unseen, or something seen which is not known to be dangerous.

Sculpin

Of the creatures you may not see are the Sculpin, or "scorpion fish," and the Stonefish. The Sculpin is found in U.S. coastal waters and camouflages itself on the bottom. In fact, its appearance is much like that of a rock or shell when lying still. Its sting is not fatal, but painful, and should be treated by running hot water directly over the wound. The Stonefish looks much like the Sculpin, but it is more dangerous. It is found mostly in the Pacific and is very difficult to spot; its camouflage makes it almost indistinguishable from the rocks and corals it inhabits. Treatment for a Stonefish sting includes hot water flushing, and the victim will also require immediate emergency care.

Stonefish

The eel is an animal you may see hiding in rocks, crevices and coral formations. One of the most common is the Moray Eel. Eels are nocturnal and will be more free-swimming at night, so there is little danger of contact. However, if disturbed while at rest inside dark enclosures where they live, eels may react by biting. Eels are normally quite shy and will avoid confrontation if possible.

Eel

Among creatures that do not appear to be dangerous at first glance are several of the phylum Coelenterata, which includes the Jellyfish and the Portuguese Man-of-War. The Coelenteratas' nematocysts force poison into a victim when touched. The sting needs to be taken care of immediately: Leave the water, leave the stingers alone, douse the wound with vinegar or ammonia, or apply a commercial anti-sting solution, and get medical attention.

The most dangerous Coelenterata is the Sea Wasp. The tentacles on the Sea Wasp can reach 33 feet (10 metres) in length. A six-inch length of tentacle has enough poison to kill an adult. If you are stung by these tentacles you will have extreme pain around the affected area. Within the first 90 minutes after the sting, the victim can become unconscious and stop breathing. Treatment

Jellyfish

Portuguese Man-of-War

for a Sea Wasp sting includes applying copious amounts of vinegar or ice to the affected area and removing the tentacles very carefully. Apply a pressure bandage of vinegar or ice, monitor the vital signs and transport the victim to the nearest emergency medical facility.

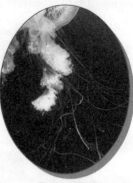

Tentacles

The Cone Shell has a venomous stinger that hides inside its shell. Though Cone Shells do not attack, stings can result from careless handling because divers mistake them for harmless sea shells. If you cannot positively identify a shell, do not pick it up. Treat Cone Shell stings by flushing with hot water and seek medical attention immediately. Cone shell stings can be deadly.

Cone Shell

The sharp spines of the Sea Urchin are a common cause of puncture wounds. Care must be used to avoid breaking off any spines in the skin. Treat the puncture by immersing it in tolerable hot water to achieve pain relief. Gently remove any visible pieces of the spine and then scrub the wound with soap and water. If the spine is near a joint, or the wound is showing signs of infection, you must receive proper medical attention.

Sea Urchin

Manta Ray

When moving on the bottom, divers should watch for the inconspicuous ray. Several of the stingrays, including the Butterfly, the Bat, the Round Ray and the Stingray, are capable of wounding an aggressive diver, or a diver who accidentally steps on one while it is inconspicuously burrowed into the sandy bottom. When disturbed or provoked they will swim away, but if attacked they will strike up with their tail and can drive a venomous barb located on the tail into an intruder. The sting will cause bleeding and swelling, and the

Stingray

poison can have serious side effects such as vomiting and faintness. If you are wounded by a ray, get out of the water, immerse the wound in hot water and get medical attention.

The Sea Snake is abundant in the Indian and Pacific Oceans, in the Persian Gulf and throughout Asia. Most species spend their entire lives in the open sea. Though they are sluggish and not aggressive, they can bite if handled or provoked. The venom of sea snakes is powerful so the victim must be taken to medical services as soon as possible to receive antivenin.

Sea Snake

A small but formidable foe is the Lionfish. It is nice to look at but carries a powerful sting. Immediate treatment is a hot water flush, and medical attention may also be required.

Another type of injury is the aggressive injury in which an animal takes a purposeful and willing part. An example of this is a shark bite. These injuries are rare.

Lionfish

There is no doubt that some sharks are unpredictable and can be dangerous, but this occurs almost exclusively when provoked.

They are fast and strong and become very excited at the smell of blood in the water. Knowing these two facts — that they can be provoked and that they are excited by blood — are what film and documentary producers have employed to manufacture the myth of the ferocious shark. You can get even the tamest of sharks to react violently by chumming the water — tossing in bucketfuls of meat, intestines, and blood. But sharks are actually quite

Nurse Shark

Sand Shark

5

graceful and can even be cowardly, often bolting away at sudden movement.

The most commonly seen sharks are the least aggressive. The Nurse and the Sand Shark are among these. More aggressive sharks include the Tiger, the Great White, the Mako, and the Hammerhead.

Another large fish, which does not quite deserve its reputation as a hostile predator is the Barracuda. While it does have a fearsome appearance and does tend to stalk, it is actually very gentle and intelligent. It may follow a diver just out of curiosity; barracudas have been known to be very friendly, in fact.

Barracuda

We have only glossed the number of potentially dangerous marine life forms. For your purposes as a diver, it is more important to know what you are likely to encounter when diving in a particular area. Many dangerous animals are indigenous to only one region.

Ask your SSI Dealer or Instructor what to look out for in their local waters, how to recognize them, how to avoid them and what to do if you are injured.

While the coral reef offers protection and food for warm water dwellers, the deeper cold water areas do the same for their inhabitants. Cold water bottom formations are mostly comprised of rock, and along some coastlines, kelp beds. Though not as colorful as the coral reefs, cold waters often offer a greater quantity of marine life with a view of some of the most exciting ocean creatures, including marine mammals such as sea lions, seals, dolphins, and whales.

The kelp forests found in coastal areas of California, Alaska and Japan, to name a few, offer very unique diving experiences. Kelp is abundant with life and is home to many of the kinds of oceangoing fish we meet most often at dinnertime: Halibut, Flounder, Sole and Turbot.

Flounder

Garibaldi

Other fish commonly seen in the kelp forests include the bright orange Garibaldi and a wide variety of rockfish.

Kelp is not difficult for the trained diver to move through if it is done slowly and carefully, without a struggle. However, a thorough orientation in kelp diving should precede any attempt at exploring this magical environment. Consult local dive stores in regions where kelp is abundant. In areas where it grows to the water's surface, the kelp forms a "bed" which can be traveled across by using a kelp crawl.

If you ever become entangled in kelp, simply stay calm, move slowly, and gradually disentangle yourself. Your buddy may be able to help.

Artificial structures such as oil rig platforms and ship wrecks serve as "reefs" in colder waters. They offer protection for smaller fish and, therefore, attract larger pelagic fish that come to feed. It is not uncommon to see Yellowtail Jacks, smaller species of tuna, bonito, mackerel, small barracuda, and possibly sharks.

Freshwater Environments

Though ocean and coastal diving is popular, there are many inland, freshwater dive experiences worth investigating. Many divers live too far inland from salt water sites to be able to dive them exclusively, so they find some very diverse and interesting dive sites nearer to home. Inland dive sites include lakes, rivers and quarry ponds, to name a few. Find out about possible dive sites in your area by talking to your SSI Dealer, your SSI Instructor and other divers from your area. You may also want to look into a Specialty Course in Limited Visibility Diving or Unique Specialty Courses, such as River Diving, that are designed to fit the local diving needs in your area.

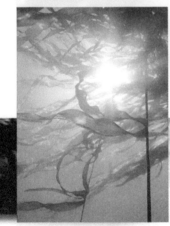

Kelp

Freshwater Life

Depending on the area of the world where you are diving, you are likely to run into one of a number of fish belonging to a few freshwater families, including Bass, Pike, Perch, Catfish, Trout, Carp, Crappie and Gar.

Fresh waters also contain cousins to the more delectable ocean inhabitants, the lobster and clam. Crayfish, commonly known as crawdad, are found in almost any type of fresh water. They are much smaller than the lobster, but are edible and considered by some to be very good. Clams can also be found in fresh water, but the only ones recommended for eating are those found in clear, fresh water.

The fresh water food chain is usually formed around floating or rooted plants, but is also abundant around fresh water ship wrecks. There are many famous wrecks in areas such as the Great Lakes of the United States. Fresh water can offer many great dive experiences.

Summary

This chapter is in no way intended to answer all your questions or address all your concerns regarding dive locations and environments. We have covered some basics here: basics of water and how it behaves and some basics about what you are likely to see when you go diving. To learn more specifics about water movement you will need to take a SSI Specialty Course in Waves, Tides and Currents.

Always work directly with your SSI Dealer and your SSI Instructor when planning a dive for a particular location. Find out about water temperatures so that you can determine exposure suit needs. Find out about local water conditions so that you can plan safe dive sites and safe entries and exits. Do not be timid about inquiring into the quality and reputation of dive expedition businesses and dive boat crews. This is your dive, and again, your comfort leads to your enjoyment. Your SSI Dealer is available to answer your questions and help you arrange diving excursions and diving vacations. These Dealers can save you much time and money, while helping prevent travel problems.

Lastly, the real sensations of diving can only be experienced in the real setting. Reading this chapter is the blueprint; scuba diving is the completed bridge to a world of discoveries. If you have imagined moving in weightless suspension over the entrancing collage of color and texture we call the coral reef, you will be awestruck the first time you experience it for real.

Section 5 Study Guide Questions

1. The surface of this planet is actually made up of very little earth. It is in fact about _____ water.

2. It is estimated that plant production in the oceans may be _____ times more than that on land. More than _____ of the oxygen is produced by marine plants. Even the photosynthesis that takes place on land requires water, which originates in the oceans.

3. For us as divers, the oceans may be playgrounds, but playgrounds are only fun and exciting if we keep them _____ and well _____.

4. The force that originally acts on the water to create tide is the gravity of the _____ and _____, primarily the _____, pulling at the side of the earth nearest the moon.

5. Near shore, the best time for diving would probably be during periods of _____ exchange of _____ between the tides.

6. Because dense, cold water tends to sink underneath warm water, layer of various temperatures are found at different depths. The boundaries between these layers are called _____.

7. You should keep in mind when freshwater diving that the temperature at the _____ may be much warmer than the temperature at your _____ _____.

8. The _____ and harder the wind blows, the _____ the waves become. The longer the fetch, the further the wave action will be extended.

9. It is important to hold on when entering the boat because while your _____ feels weightless in the water, as soon as you emerge from the water it will weigh you down and you may instantaneously feel the full weight of your body and equipment transferred to your _____ .

10. Take these precautions in case you accidentally slip back into the water: Keep your mask in place so you can _____, your regulator or snorkel in place so you can _____, and your BC inflated so you can _____ .

11. When entering or exiting from shore, the diver's primary concern is to avoid being knocked down and buffeted by _____ and _____ .

12. Any time waves reach shoreline, the water must return to sea. This returning water creates a back current, or _____ _____ .

13. Any time you do find yourself facing into a rip current, turn and swim at a _____ _____ or _____ to it until you catch a shoreward water movement, or at least move out of the main force of the current.

14. In _____ _____ you simply float along with the current, and so does the boat. when you surface, the boat picks you up.

15. Many dive sites throughout the world are considered _____ _____ and are protected by law. This protection helps keep these dive sites in pristine condition by _____ the coral and other aquatic marine life from hunters and collectors.

16. Sea stars, brittle stars, sea urchins, sand dollars, and sea cucumbers all belong to the group of animals known as the _____ .

17. The _____, fishes and mammals, are well
    known and are the most visible life forms in the open waters.

18. The creatures capable of inflicting injury will do so only
    _____. They will react when surprised by
    being _____ or having their territory invaded, or
    when taunted or molested.

19. There is no doubt that some sharks are _____
    and can be dangerous — but almost exclusively when provoked.

20. Depending on the area of the world where you are diving, you are
    likely to run into one of a number of fish belonging to a few
    _____ _____, including
    Bass, Pike, Perch, Catfish, Trout, Carp, Crappie and Gar.

SCUBA SCHOOLS
INTERNATIONAL

Your Scuba Diving Experiences and Beyond

"It seems to me we can never give up longing and wishing while we are thoroughly alive. There are certain things we feel to be beautiful and good, and we must hunger after them."

— George Eliot

Your Open Water Dives

After completing steps 1 and 2 of the certification process, you are ready for step 3—open water dives! In this step you perform all the skills you learned and practiced in the pool or confined water. An instructor evaluates your ability and comfort while you explore the underwater world.

There are two ways in which you can complete the open water dives. The first is with your local SSI training facility, and the other is by referral. To select which method is best for you, talk to your instructor.

With Your SSI Dealer

Your Dealer will have a schedule of open water training dates. Most likely, they will offer local and dive travel options. Both options are equal from an educational standpoint. The differences are cost, timeliness and logistics.

Local training is convenient and affordable and you get to sample local diving conditions. If your time and budget allow it, dive travel is a wonderful introduction to open water diving. You will experience clear water, abundant marine life and the other pleasures of a dive vacation.

Section 6 Objectives

After completing this section you will understand:

- The reasons you should complete referrals through the Universal Referral Network,

- How to maintain proficiency with scuba skills,

- The SSI Continuing Education Ratings,

- Why experience is required for SSI Continuing Education Ratings,

- Why having Specialty and Continuing Education cards are important,

- The requirements to earn SSI Levels of Recognition and

- The types of training included in the SSI Dive Control Specialist course.

Some students become very comfortable with a certain instructor and want to complete the whole course with that person. This is only possible if you complete your open water dives with your original instructor.

By Referral

If you cannot complete your open water dives through your SSI Dealer, your instructor can refer you to another instructor.

Scuba Schools International is a founding member of the Universal Referral Program (URP), an industry wide effort to make referrals convenient for divers. The International Diving Educators Association (IDEA), National Association of Underwater Instructors (NAUI), Professional Diving Instructors Corporation (PDIC) and YMCA Scuba Program also use the Universal Referral Program.

Here are a few tips to a successful referral:

◆ URP paperwork is only valid for 30 days,

◆ If you have a physician's approval, take a copy of the signed medical form,

◆ Call ahead to make sure the resort is part of the Universal Referral Program network,

◆ Make sure your referral instructor signs your URP paperwork before you go home,

◆ The URP referral instructor should issue you a temporary card and

◆ Your instructor at home will issue your SSI Certification Card when you return. So there is no need to purchase another card at the resort.

Please be advised that if you go outside the Universal Referral Program network, it is likely that instructors will not accept your referral paperwork. In fact, before you can go on open water dives, you may have to complete new waivers and a new medical history, learn new dive tables, retake a written exam, and perform skills again in the pool. After completing open water dives, they will order you a non-SSI certification card. For this, you will likely pay additional fees.

Luckily, it is easy to avoid this unnecessary duplication of effort and expense. Simply go to a resort that is part of the Universal Referral Program network. Check www.UniversalReferral.com for more information and a list of participants.

1 Complete a Medical History

2 Complete a New Waiver

3 Relearn the Dive Tables

4 Retake the Written Exam

5 Review Skills in the Pool

6 Pay More Fees

7 Receive a Non-SSI Certification Card

College Credit for Scuba Courses

Divers in the United States can earn college credit for scuba courses, thanks to Scuba Schools International's association with the American Council on Education (ACE).

ACE has recommended four SSI courses for college credit. They are

◆ SSI Open Water Diver,

◆ SSI Diver Stress & Rescue,

◆ SSI Dive Control Specialist and

◆ SSI Open Water Instructor.

To earn credit, you must have an official transcript from Scuba Schools International. Official transcripts verify to the college or university that the course was taken and passed. Ask your Dealer to order official transcripts from SSI USA, or visit **www.ssiusa.com** and go to the Diver Services area.

If you have friends who are SSI divers, they are also eligible to earn college credit. They can get official transcripts for SSI courses they took all the way back to 1991.

Your Diving Adventures

After you have earned your SSI Open Water Diver certification, your diving adventures can officially begin! Many new divers have the same questions. How do I get started? Whom do I go diving with? Where are the good diving sites? This section outlines how you can make the most of your training, your equipment and your opportunities for adventure.

Finding Dive Buddies

The first step is finding other people who share your passion for diving. Dive buddies show you the local dive spots, as well as share tips on equipment and special techniques necessary for certain dive sites. They can share their favorite places for dive vacations. They motivate and inspire you to get out and go diving.

Since you are a new diver, where do you find dive buddies? Start with the people in your class. Your SSI Dealer is another great place to look. Most facilities have "buddy boards" that list other people who want to go diving. Many facilities sponsor local dives where you can meet other divers.

Joining a Dive and Travel Club is ...

A great way to stay involved with diving, meet other divers, learn about local dive spots and go on individual or group dive trips.

Throughout the world, SSI Training Facilities offer SSI Club Aquarius. For a nominal membership fee, you get outstanding benefits such as air fills, a club newsletter, discounts on travel and many others. Your local chapter may offer even more benefits. Ask your SSI Instructor or Dealer about joining Club Aquarius today.

Diving at Home

No matter where you live, you can have fun diving. It does not matter if you live near an ocean, lake, river or quarry, underwater adventure and exploration await you. Local diving can mean discovering wrecks, collecting game, watching fish or relaxing with your friends on a Saturday morning dive.

Let's face it. Dive travel is great, but most divers enjoy it on an infrequent basis.

Local diving is an opportunity to have fun with your dive buddies, use your equipment and gain valuable diving experience anytime you want.

It is possible that you will need further training to develop the knowledge and skills necessary for local diving. It is also possible you may need additional diving equipment. Ask your SSI Dealer about the diving opportunities near your home.

Diving on Vacation

Dive travel is a special treat. For many divers, dive travel means a relaxing vacation to tropical islands, nice hotels, good food and romantic evenings. For other divers it means adventure travel to the remote corners of the world where primitive conditions equate to pristine dive sites rarely seen by humans.

Divers are friendly, active, adventurous people. We encourage you to look for and take advantage of every opportunity to use your training and equipment to become a serious diver.

KNOWLEDGE SKILLS

DIVER DIAMOND SSI
SCUBA SCHOOLS INTERNATIONAL

EQUIPMENT EXPERIENCE

The explosion of dive travel has created a multitude of options for divers that can meet anyone's expectations, budget and time considerations.

To help sort through the dizzying array of options, ask your SSI Dealer to help you plan your next dive trip. They are the dive travel specialists and they keep up with the top destinations, hotels, liveaboards and dive sites.

If individual travel is more your style, your SSI Dealer can help with that as well. Many have their own travel agencies or are connected to large dive travel companies.

Group trips through your SSI Dealer are a relaxing, hassle-free way to travel. They take care of the accommodations, dive boats, transfers, dive equipment, luggage and often the food as well. All you do is show up and have a good time with the rest of the group.

Getting the Family Involved

Diving is an awesome sport because people of all ages and abilities can have fun diving together. This means the whole family can get involved in scuba diving.

Scuba Schools International offers special certifications for children. Children from 12 to 15 can earn a junior certification that allows them to dive when accompanied by an adult. Children 10 to 11 years old are eligible for a special junior certification that allows them to dive with an adult, but only in shallow water.

Below age 10, Scuba Schools International recommends Scuba Rangers, an organization dedicated to involving children in scuba diving.

Scuba Rangers is a "Way Cool Kids' Club" where children dive in a pool, attend club meetings, and become better kids. For more information, visit **www.ScubaRangers.com**.

Staying Proficient

Even though your certification is valid for a lifetime, it is important to keep your scuba skills proficient. The only way to stay proficient is by diving. While there is no magic number, a good rule of thumb is to dive at least four to five times per year.

If you have not been diving in a year or more, Scuba Schools International recommends that you update your skills with an SSI Diveleader. This is called a Scuba Skills Update program, and it consists of reviewing basic knowledge, skills and equipment handling techniques. Your instructor will adhere an official decal and sign the tab in your SSI Total DiveLog.

Many dive destinations require that you have recent diving experience. The Scuba Skills Update tab in your Total DiveLog shows at-a-glance that you have kept your skills proficient.

Keep Learning

To be a serious diver, it is important to keep learning. A great way to do this is to visit your SSI Dealer. They keep up-to-date on everything that is happening in the sport regarding education, equipment, local diving and dive travel.

Also, check the Scuba Schools International web sites for regional information.

Another way to acquire more knowledge is by subscribing to diving publications. There are many to choose from and since they all have a different style and focus, you can read them each month without an overlap.

Beyond Open Water Diver

Your Open Water Diver certification is the starting point of an incredible journey. Think of the SSI Education System as your road map, with pathways for training and experience. The staff at your SSI Dealer are your seasoned guides, always available to help you accomplish your personal dreams and goals.

Responsible Diver Code

My responsible diving duties include:

1. Diving within the limits of my ability and training.

2. Evaluating the conditions before every dive and making sure they fit my personal capabilities.

3. Being familiar with and checking my equipment before and during every dive.

4. Respecting the buddy system and its advantages.

5. Accepting the responsibility for my own safety on every dive.

6. Being environmentally conscious on every dive.

The only question you need to answer is, "How far do I want to go?"

Continuing Your Adventure

Learning about specialty activities, such as diving on wrecks, fish watching, photography and night diving, is the next logical step in your adventure. Specialties give purpose, add challenge and open up new areas of interest to diving.

Specialty activities can be combined to open up limitless possibilities for adventure. For instance, you could combine nitrox diving and photography, navigation and wreck diving or dry suit diving and boat diving.

Specialty Courses

The easiest way to get started in any specialty activity is to take a specialty course.

SSI Specialty Courses are fun, practical and educational. The same 1-2-3 approach used in your Open Water Diver course applies to specialty courses.

Step 1 is academics, which is often done in home study format. With most SSI specialty courses, the exam is optional.

Step 2 involves an optional pool session for basic skill review and practice.

Step 3 consists of two open water dives, where you learn practical, real-world skills and techniques from experienced and knowledgeable instructors. They want you to enjoy the activity as much as they do and to do it right. Most go beyond the basics and share their secrets for diving better and smarter. It is a fun, exciting experience.

Scuba Schools International offers a large menu of specialty courses. A menu allows you to pursue whatever diving adventures you want because you can select the courses that interest you.

Menu of SSI Specialty Courses

- Computer Diving
- Deep Diving
- Dry Suit Diving
- Navigation
- Enriched Air Nitrox
- Wreck Diving
- Diver Stress & Rescue
- Boat Diving
- Equipment Techniques
- Search & Recovery
- Underwater Photography
- Waves, Tides & Currents
- Night/Limited Visibility Diving

KNOWLEDGE SKILLS
DIVER DIAMOND
SSI
SCUBA SCHOOLS INTERNATIONAL
EQUIPMENT EXPERIENCE

Specialty Course Tab. Located in your SSI DiveLog, this tab shows all SSI specialty courses you have taken. As you pursue SSI Continuing Education Ratings this becomes important.

Specialty Course Cards. Cards are available for every SSI specialty course. Many dive resorts are now requiring proof of specialty training to participate in specialty dives such as deep, night and nitrox. When you complete specialty courses, ask your SSI Dealer to order your cards so you have verification of training when you need it and personal recognition for the courses you took.

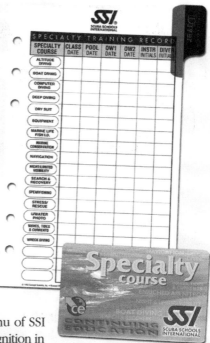

Continuing Education Ratings

As you accumulate specialties from the menu of SSI courses, you can earn special rewards and recognition in the SSI Education System.

In our system, you combine specialty courses with logged dives to earn SSI Continuing Education Ratings. It is like earning a college degree; you select the degree you want— Bachelor's, Master's or Ph.D.— and take the courses necessary to get that degree.

SSI Standards

Scuba Schools International has the highest standards in the industry for continuing education because we require additional logged dives to earn Continuing Education Ratings. Comparing the SSI Advanced Open Water Diver rating to those from other organizations is like comparing apples to oranges. SSI advanced divers are more comfortable, more confident and have more ability. Most importantly, they have more fun!

Higher continuing education requirement is yet another example of SSI's commitment to quality. When we say we have a passion for serious diving and serious fun, we mean it.

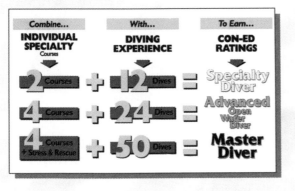

There are three SSI Continuing Education Ratings:

1. Specialty Diver

2. Advanced Open Water Diver

3. Master Diver

To earn SSI Continuing Education Ratings you must meet two requirements:

1. Training — specialty courses

2. Experience — logged dives

Training Requirement. Every SSI specialty course listed on page 6-9 qualifies for Continuing Education Ratings. So how do you select which ones you want to take?

Some SSI Training Facilities offer a menu of specialty courses. The advantage is you get to select the courses you want and take them at your pace.

Other SSI Facilities offer continuing education programs. These are preselected groups of popular specialty courses that prepare you for the type of diving in your local area. It usually takes two days of diving to complete this type of program.

Ask for a personal orientation with an SSI Instructor to define your options and help you make choices.

Experience Requirement. The experience requirement makes you a very comfortable, truly advanced diver, because you put your skills to use in the real world.

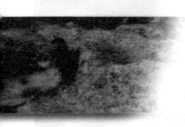

Amazingly, Scuba Schools International is the only organization with an experience requirement, even though it produces more confident, comfortable divers.

To meet the experience requirement, simply record your dives in your SSI Total DiveLog. Every dive you make counts, even training dives. When you reach the Level of Experience necessary for the rating you want, have a staff member at your SSI Dealer verify your accomplishment. If you are on a dive trip, the SSI facility you are diving with can also verify it.

Record Keeping. There are several tools in your SSI Total DiveLog that document your progress in meeting the requirements. Your Advanced Open Water Instructor will handle the recordkeeping.

◆ Training Pages — Located in the Training section (see page 6-10).

◆ Specialty Course Tab — Documents all specialty courses you have taken.

◆ Experience Sign-off Pages — Located at the end of every section in your SSI Total DiveLog. For a complete description, see Levels of Experience on page 6-15.

Continuing Education Cards. After you have met the training and experience requirements, have your SSI Dealer order your SSI Continuing Education Card. The card is important because more and more dive resorts are requiring advanced cards to go on advanced dives. If you have any aspirations of dive leadership, advanced certifications are required. Ask your SSI Dealer to order cards for the Continuing Education Ratings you complete.

SSI SPECIALTY DIVER

Verification

To obtain your SSI Specialty Diver card, fill out the "Diver Information" portion below. Take this DiveLog to your local SSI Authorized Dealer for verification and they will order your card.

Diver Information

▲ NAME   ▲ DATE

▲ SPECIALTY DIVER CERTIFICATION CARD NUMBER

Store Verification

"We hereby verify that the holder of this dive log has met or exceeded all accepted SSI standards and completed all SSI requirements — including 2 or more SSI Specialty Courses and at least 12 open water dives — and is qualified as an 'SSI Specialty Diver.'"

▲ INSTRUCTOR   ▲ NUMBER   ▲ DATE

▲ SSI AUTHORIZED DEALER

Frequently Asked Questions

Q **A**

How does SSI's Advanced Program compare with others?

SSI's Advanced Program is a menu of in-depth specialty courses. This allows you to select your favorite specialty activities and become proficient and comfortable with them. Other programs consist of predefined sample dives, where you get to try a variety of activities, but you do not develop proficiency or comfort.

Q **A**

Do I have to take all the specialty courses at once?

No. For instance, with the Advanced Open Water Diver rating you can take specialty courses from four different instructors. The final instructor issues your advanced card.

Q **A**

Can I get SSI specialty course cards in addition to my continuing education cards?

Yes. For example, if you complete an Advanced Open Water Diver (AOWD) program with four specialty courses, you are entitled to five different cards (the AOWD and four specialties).

Q **A**

What if I complete the training but do not have enough dives for my card?

That is ok. Have your instructor issue an SSI *Continuing Education Student Individual Registration (SIR) Form*. It comes with a temporary card to use while you complete the experience requirement. When you log enough dives, have the form verified at an SSI Dealer, and send it to SSI for processing.

Q **A**

What dives count toward the experience requirement?

All dives, including entry-level training dives, specialty training dives and fun dives.

Q **A**

Why are SSI's requirements so much higher than other organization's?

With other organizations, you can earn an "advanced" card with as few as *nine dives* —all under an instructor's supervision! That is not our style. While training accelerates the learning process, *experience* is the difference between "beginner" and "advanced."

Sharing Your Adventure

Dive leadership is an extension of the training path. If you have an interest in leading dives, teaching divers or making a career out of scuba diving, talk to your SSI Instructor about a Personal Orientation.

Dive Control Specialist

SSI Dive Control Specialists are really two ratings in one. DiveCons combine the duties of dive masters and assistant instructors and is the highest entry level leadership program in the industry. DiveCons work on dive boats, dive resorts and retail shops.

Open Water Instructor

SSI Open Water Instructors teach entry-level scuba courses.

Advanced Open Water Instructor

SSI Advanced Open Water Instructors teach specialty courses.

Dive Control Specialist Instructor

SSI Dive Control Specialist Instructors teach Dive Control Specialist courses. Dive Control Specialist Instructors have made a high level of commitment to Scuba Schools International.

Instructor Trainer

SSI Instructor Trainers teach Instructor Training Courses. An Instructor Certifier must complete the Instructor Evaluation, the final set of exams. Instructor Trainers are individuals who have been teaching divers for many years and have a great deal of experience in the diving industry.

Instructor Certifier

SSI Instructor Certifiers teach Instructor Training Courses, and they can conduct Instructor Evaluations. Instructor Certifiers are individuals who have made the highest level of commitment to Scuba Schools International and are some of the finest instructors in the diving industry.

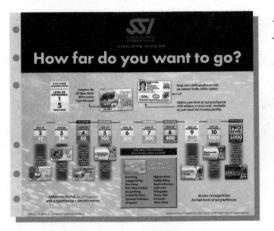

Lifetime of Adventure

Serious divers know that training accelerates the learning process, but there is no substitute for experience.

Every time you dive you are adding experience and becoming a better diver. Since diving is something you can enjoy for the rest of your life, your ability can progress as far as you want it to.

Levels of Experience

As you gain experience, it is important to communicate what level of diver you are. After all, no one wants to be a beginner forever! Scuba Schools International supports 11 Levels of Experience, representing a progression from beginning diver to professional. Each level is defined by a range of dives.

It is easy to upgrade to a new Level of Experience by visiting an SSI Dealer. A staff member simply verifies the number of dives recorded in your SSI Total DiveLog.

5 OR MORE LOGGED DIVES

12 OR MORE LOGGED DIVES

24 OR MORE LOGGED DIVES

50 OR MORE LOGGED DIVES

The components of the SSI Experience Program include:

◆ **SSI Total DiveLog.** The pages are divided into sections corresponding to the Levels of Experience, with tabs separating the sections.

◆ **SSI Levels of Experience Decals.** These indicate your level and are applied to Verification Pages and certification cards.

◆ **SSI Verification Pages.** After you log all the dives in a section of your Total DiveLog, you will find a Verification Page at the end. A staff member at the training facility completes this page (see page 6-12).

◆ **SSI Certification Cards.** The back of every SSI certification card lists your number of dives. You can upgrade your certification card with an Experience Decal, or you can order a new card with your current number of dives.

◆ **SSI Embosser.** To make everything official, your SSI Dealer will stamp your Verification Page with an official SSI Embosser.

Levels of Recognition

When you achieve a significant Level of Experience, you deserve recognition. That is why, in 1992, Scuba Schools International created the first cards in the industry to recognize divers for their experience. No training beyond Open Water Diver is necessary and any brand of certification qualifies.

SSI Levels of Recognition can be earned for major milestones of Level 5 (100 dives), Level 9 (500 dives), Level 10 (1000 dives) and Pro Level (5000 dives).

We like to think of Century Divers, Gold^{500} Divers, Platinum^{1000} Divers and Platinum Pro^{5000} Divers as "the world's most elite water explorers." They all share the same qualities: dedication, commitment, love of adventure and a passion for diving.

The list of Platinum Pro^{5000} Divers reads like a "who's who" of diving, consisting of the world's finest photographers, scientists, retailers, resort operators, educators and manufacturers. Such notables as Jacques and Jean Michael Cousteau, Sylvia Earle, Eugene Clark, Steven Frink and Zale Perry are Platinum Pros.

The SSI Recognition Program reflects the core values of our organization, our belief in diving experience and our desire to recognize everyone who really supports our sport.

How Much is 5000 Dives?

To put 5,000 dives in perspective, you would have to dive 500 times a year for 10 years, or 100 times a year for 50 years to earn a Platinum Pro^{5000} Diver rating! Only a longtime, dedicated industry professional has a shot at earning it.

Platinum
PRO^{5000}
Diver

THE WORLD'S MOST ELITE WATER EXPLORERS

Platinum
PRO^{5000}
Diver

SSI
SCUBA SCHOOLS
INTERNATIONAL

PRO LEVEL:
5000 OPEN WATER DIVES

Sharing the Freedom of Diving

The Platinum Pro Foundation is an independent, nonprofit group formed in 1997. The Foundation's mission is to help individuals with physical challenges experience the freedom of scuba diving, as well as increase the awareness and use of Adaptive Scuba programs throughout the world.

The Platinum Pro Foundation is the legacy of Platinum Pro^{5000} Divers. Their hope is to involve the physically challenged in the freedom and mobility that the underwater world offers.

By supporting the use of Adaptive Scuba training and specific programs like Cody Unser's Great Scuba Adventure, the foundation is changing the lives one dive at a time.

Scuba Schools International supports the Platinum Pro Foundation and we encourage you to support this valuable cause as well. If you want to make a donation or inquire about volunteer opportunities, ask your SSI Instructor or Dealer, or visit **www.WaterExplorer.com**.

Cody Unser

Platinum Pro Foundation

Bringing the freedom of diving to the physically challenged.
WaterExplorer.com

Section 6 Study Guide Questions

1. There are two ways in which you can complete the open water dives. The first is with your _____ _____ _____, and the other is by _____. To select which method is best for you, talk to your instructor.

2. Divers in the United States can earn _____ _____ for scuba courses, thanks to Scuba Schools International's association with the American Council on Education (ACE).

3. Most facilities have "_____ _____" that list other people who want to go diving.

4. No matter where you live, you can have fun diving. It does not matter if you live near an _____, lake, _____ or quarry, underwater adventure and exploration awaits you.

5. Local diving is an opportunity to have fun with your dive buddies, use your _____ and gain valuable diving _____ anytime you want.

6. For many divers, _____ _____ means a relaxing vacation to tropical islands, nice hotels, good food and romantic evenings. For other divers it means adventure travel to the remote corners of the world where primitive conditions equate to pristine _____ _____ rarely seen by humans.

7. Group trips through your _____ _____ are a relaxing, hassle-free way to travel. They take care of the _____, dive boats, transfers, dive equipment, luggage and often the food as well.

8. Diving is an awesome sport because people of all _____ and _____ can have fun diving together. This means that the whole _____ can get involved in scuba diving.

9. Even though your certification is valid for a _____, it is important to keep your scuba skills proficient. The only way to stay proficient is by _____. While there is no magic number, a good rule of thumb is to dive at least _____ to _____ times per year.

10. Many dive destinations require that you have recent diving _____. The _____ _____ _____ tab in your Total DiveLog shows at-a-glance that you have kept your skills proficient.

11. Learning about _____ activities, such as diving on wrecks, fish watching, photography and night diving, is the next logical step in your adventure.

12. Specialty activities can be combined to open up _____ possibilities for adventure. For instance, you could _____ nitrox diving and photography, navigation and wreck diving, or dry suit diving and boat diving.

13. Scuba Schools International offers a large _____ of _____ _____. A menu allows you to pursue whatever diving adventures _____ want, because you can select the courses that interest you.

14. Comparing the SSI Advanced Open Water Diver rating to those from other organizations is like comparing apples to oranges. SSI advanced divers are more _____, more _____ and have more _____. Most importantly, they have more fun!

15. Amazingly, Scuba Schools International is the only organization with an _____ _____, even though it produces more confident, comfortable divers.

16. If you have an interest in _____ dives, _____ divers, or making a career out of scuba diving, talk to your SSI Instructor about a Personal Orientation.

17. SSI Dive Control Specialists are really two ratings in one. DiveCons combine the duties of _____ _____ and _____ _____, and is the highest entry level leadership program in the industry.

18. It is easy to upgrade to a new _____ of _____ by visiting an SSI Dealer. A staff member simply verifies the number of dives recorded in your SSI Total DiveLog.

19. SSI _____ of _____ can be earned for major milestones of Level 5 (100 dives), Level 9 (500 dives), Level 10 (100 dives) and Pro Level (5000 dives).

20. To keep our sport strong, it is important to cultivate the next generation of divers. The _____ _____ _____ is an independent, non-profit group formed in 1997 with a mission of educating children about the waters of the world.

Photo Credits

Rusty Berry. Pg. 6-Title Page, *Garibaldis*; Pg. 5-33, *Garibaldi*; Pg. 5-29, *Jellyfish*.

Burleson Scuba. Pg. 5-24, *Fire Coral (lower)*; Pg. 5-29, *Stonefish*.

Richard Buttenshaw. Pg. 5-22, *Coral Polyps*; Pg. 5-24, *Christmas Tree Worm (lower)*; Pg. 5-25 *Hermit Crab*; Pg. 5-30, *Cone Shell, Stingray*.

Frank Best Campbell. Pg. 1-17, *Fish on Reef*; Pg. 2-12, *Angel on Reef*; Pg. 5-25, *Crab*.

Larry Cox. Pg. 3-14, *Crab*; Pg. 5-24, *Sea Fan (left)*; Pg. 5-31, *Sand Shark*.

Martin Denison. Pages 1-37, 2-2, 3-5, 3-26, 4-9, *Masked Butterfly*.

Black Durgeon Inn. Pg. 3-11, *Long Nose Hawkfish*; Pg. 5-4, *Parrot Fish*; Pg. 5-25, *Squid*; Pg. 5-30, *Lionfish*; Pg. 5-33, *Kelp (upper)*; Pages Intro-6, 1-8, 1-39, 2-1, 6-2, *Juvenile Tang*.

Keith Ibsen. Pages 1-15, 2-3, 2-29, 3-4, 4-2, *Long Snout Butterfly*; Pages 1-34, 2-25, 3-22, *Wrasse*; Pages 1-24, 1-29, 2-15, 2-29, *Varying Fish on Reef*.

Paolo Lilla. Pg. 3-24, *Orange Polyps*; Pg. 3-26, *Jellyfish*; Pg. 5-14, *Fish on Reef*; Pg. 5-25, *Lobster, Flamingo Tongue*; Pg. 5-26 *Sea Urchin*; Pg. 5-28, *Groupers (2)*; Pages 1-15, 2-18, 3-12, 4-6, *Grouper*; Pg. 5-29, *Eel (lower)*; Pages 1-34, 2-1, 3-25, 4-22, *Scrawled File*; Pages 1-38, 2-30, 3-20, 4-21, *Spotted Puffer*; Pages 1-31, 2-11, 2-30, 3-26, 5-28, 6-1, *Squirrel Fish*; Pages 1-33, 2-11, 3-26, *Spotted File*; Pages 1-31, 2-2, 2-3, 3-30, 4-16, *Regal Angel*; Pages Intro-2, 1-8, 1-40, 2-7, 4-8, *Blue Angel*; Pages Intro-5, 1-38, 2-16, 3-34, 4-11, *Desjardin Sail Fin Tang*; Pages Intro-7, 1-40, 3-19, 4-3, *Juvenile Queen Angel*; Pages 1-33, 1-39, 3-9, 5-28, *Queen Trigger*; Pages 1-33, 2-2, 2-24, 3-8, 4-3, *Starfish*.

Rick Murchison. Pages Intro-6, 1-10, 2-25, 4-6, *Barred Hamlet*; Pages 1-25, 2-20, 2-21, 3-15, 4-16, *French Angel*.

Jeff Powelson. Pg. 4-25, *Seahorse*; Pg. 4-27, *Shipwreck Dive*.

Kelley Scarzafava. Pages 3-1, 5-32, *Barracuda*; Pg. 5-23, *Staghorn Coral*; Pg. 5-24, *Lettuce Leaf Coral*; Pg. 5-24, *Red Coral*; Pg. 5-25, *Sea Star*; Pg. 5-27, *Grey Angel, Emperor Angel, Spotfin Butterfly*; Pg. 5-29, *Sculpin*; Pg. 5-30, *Sea Urchin, Tentacles*; Pg. 5-31, *Nurse Shark*; Pg. 5-33, *Kelp (lower)*; Pg. 6-9, *Boat Diving*.

SSI Australia. Pages 1-25, 2-7, 2-28, 2-29, 3-9, 4-2, *Square Spot Anthias*; Pages 1-32, 2-29, 3-32, 6-15, *Banded Angel*.

Vernantius Xavier. Pg. 5-23, *Elkhorn Coral*; Pg. 5-24, *Star Coral, Christmas Tree Worm (upper), Fire Coral (upper)*; Pg. 5-25, *Octupus*; Pg. 5-26, *Sea Cucumber*; Pg. 5-27, *French Angel*; Pg. 5-28, *Glasseye*.

Amy Young. Pg. 5-24, *Feather Duster*.

Glossary of Diving Terms

Actual Time (AT). The actual amount of time a diver spent under water on a repetitive scuba dive.

Air Embolism. When a diver fails to exhale on ascent, overexpansion of the lungs can create a condition in which air bubbles are forced into the circulatory system which may form a blockage of the flow of blood to body tissues such as the brain.

Air Sharing. An out-of-air situation in which a donor provides a needer an air source either by passing the primary or secondary regulator and then breathing off the other, or by passing the donor's primary regulator back and forth between donor and needer, or by providing the needer with an independent air system.

Air Sharing Ascent. An out-of-air ascent after air sharing has been established, and which can be aided by one or both buoyancy compensators.

Alternate Air Source. A second air source carried by the diver to be used for air sharing, or in the event the primary air source fails; may come in the form of an alternate second stage, an independent system such as a pony bottle, or as part of the power inflator system.

Alternate Second-Stage. An additional second-stage. Also known as alternate air source.

Altitude Dive. Any dive more than 1000 feet (300 metres) above sea level. The U.S. Navy Dive Tables are not accurate above 1000 feet; special altitude tables must be used.

Ambient Pressure. The total pressure surrounding the diver at a given depth. The sum of the air pressure and water pressure.

Atmosphere By Convention. the pressure exerted at sea level by a column of air 64 miles (103 km) high and 1 inch (25 mm) square (abbreviated as ATM).

Atmospheric Pressure. The pressure exerted by 1 ATM of air at sea level, expressed as 14.7 pounds per square inch (1 bar).

Bends, the. A colloquial term for decompression sickness which is derived from the bent position a victim may take due to pain in the joints.

Bottom Time. The amount of elapsed time from the start of your descent, to the time you begin your direct ascent back to the surface.

Buoyancy Compensator (BC). A device worn by a diver used to regulate buoyancy under water or as a surface flotation device. It should be equipped with an oral inflator, power inflator, and dump valve mechanism.

Buoyant Ascent. An ascent aided by inflation of the buoyancy compensator.

Certification Card. An identification card that is achieved by completing a diver certification course, and which is required in order to rent diving equipment or purchase compressed air, and participate in trips and activities available only to certified divers.

Compass. An instrument used for determining direction under water using the earth's magnetic field.

Compressed Air. Air that is purified and condensed to greater than atmospheric pressure through the use of an air compressor.

Corals. Colonial animals that lay down a skeleton of limestone and harbor a colorful microscopic plant life.

Crustaceans. Arthropods, which are usually aquatic, with a segmented body and paired, jointed limbs—lobsters and crabs, for example.

Cylinder. A hollow metal (aluminum or steel) high-pressure cylinder which is sealed with a retaining valve, and is used to carry compressed air under water.

Decompression Dive. A dive that exceeds the no-decompression time limits of the U.S. Navy Dive Tables, thus requiring planned decompression stops to eliminate excess nitrogen accumulated during the dive.

Decompression Illness. A term which describes both overexpansion injuries, including arterial gas embolism (AGE), and decompression sickness (DCS) for purposes of treatment.

Decompression Sickness. A condition resulting from inadequate release of excess nitrogen absorbed during a dive.

Depth. The deepest point reached during the dive, no matter how briefly you stayed there.

Depth Gauge. A pressure-sensitive instrument used to determine depth under water; may include a maximum depth indicator.

Dive Computer. An instrument which electronically calculates a diver's no-decompression limits and decompression requirements on a single dive or series of dives, in addition to providing other information such as depth, bottom time, surface interval time, and proper ascent rate.

Dive Tables. Tables created by the U.S. Navy which provide information to the diver on nitrogen absorption based on depth and bottom time. Allows the diver to plan no-decompression dives, and repetitive dives.

Doppler Limits. More conservative recommended no-decompression time limits at depth than the U.S. Navy time limits, based on Doppler Ultrasound Research.

Dry Suit. An exposure suit used in colder waters which prevents water entry through seals at the neck and wrists.

Emergency Swimming Ascent. A swimming ascent to the surface under stressful or emergency conditions, where the diver releases the weight system upon reaching the surface to achieve maximum positive buoyancy.

Emergency Buoyant Ascent. A swimming ascent performed in an out-of-air situation where the diver releases the weight system at depth to achieve immediate positive buoyancy.

Equalization. The process of injecting a greater amount of gas into an air space so that the pressure inside the space is the same as pressure outside or surrounding the space.

Exposure Suit. A diving suit that is worn to protect the diver from exposure to the elements (sun, abrasion, cold). Also known as dry suit, wet suit, lycra dive suit.

Fins. Footwear worn by a scuba diver or snorkeler to substantially increase the power and efficiency of the kicking motion. Fins reduce the amount of energy needed to swim a certain distance.

First-Stage. The part of the regulator system that is attached to the cylinder valve, and reduces the pressure of the compressed air from the cylinder to approximately 100-150 psi (7-10 bar) over ambient pressure.

Group Designation Letter. The letter assigned after a dive which indicates the amount of residual nitrogen remaining in the diver's tissues.

Hyperventilation. Rapid, shallow, sometimes uncontrolled breathing which is often stress or fear induced, and results in carbon dioxide buildup causing lightheadedness and an out-of-air feeling.

Hypothermia. A condition that occurs when the body's core temperature drops below the normal temperature of 98.6°F (37°C). Symptoms include confusion, bluing of the skin, rigidity, and loss of coordination.

Hypoxia. Deficiency in the amount of oxygen reaching bodily tissues; oxygen starvation.

Hyperbaric Chamber. A chamber which can be pressurized and is used to treat air embolism, decompression sickness, and other overexpansion problems.

Independent Air Source. A small, additional air bottle that is carried by the diver for use in an out-of-air situation. Also known as alternate air source, pony bottle.

Inflator-Integrated Air Source. An extra second stage built into the buoyancy compensator inflator hose, or integrated into the power inflator mechanism. Also known as alternate air source.

Instrument Console. A console that usually consists of the depth and pressure gauge, and may include a compass, timing device and diving computer; attached to the first stage of the regulator via the pressure gauge.

Invertebrate. An animal which lacks a backbone or spinal column.

Mask. Diving equipment worn over the eyes and nose to provide an air pocket for better vision and equalization of pressure.

Negative Buoyancy. The tendency or capacity for a diver to sink when immersed in water.

Neutral Buoyancy. The tendency or capacity for a diver to neither sink nor float when immersed in water.

No-Decompression Dive. Any dive that can be made to a certain depth for a maximum amount of time so that a direct ascent can be made to the surface; a dive that does not require decompression stops in order to reduce excess nitrogen.

No-Decompression Limits. Maximum specified times at given depths from which decompression stops are not required upon return to the surface as designated on the dive tables.

Oral Inflator. An inflation device on the buoyancy compensator which allows the BC to be inflated by placing it in the diver's mouth and using air from the lungs.Overexpansion Injuries Injury caused by air escaping from the lungs during ascent because of failure to exhale on ascent after breathing compressed air. Also known as air embolism, mediastinal emphysema, pneumothorax, subcutaneous emphysema.

Pelagic. Living in open seas rather than waters adjacent to land or inland waters.

Positive Buoyancy. The tendency or capacity for a diver to float when immersed in water.

Power Inflator. A device on a buoyancy compensator which is attached to the low pressure port on the first stage of the regulator, and allows quick inflation by using air from the cylinder.

Proper Weighting. The amount of weight required to keep a diver neutrally buoyant throughout a dive. This includes being able to descend below the surface at the beginning of the dive, remain neutral during the dive, and stay neutral at the end of the dive when the cylinder may become more buoyant due to low cylinder pressure.

Regulator. An apparatus which is attached to the air supply (cylinder) and is activated by inhalation; consists of a first-stage and second-stage. Also known as demand regulator.

Repetitive Dive. Any dive started within 10 minutes to 12 hours after a previous scuba dive.

Residual Time (RT). Excessive nitrogen pressure still residual in the diver at the beginning of a repetitive dive, expressed in minutes of exposure at the planned repetitive dive depth.

Safety Stop. An added safety measure of 3 to 5 minutes at 10 to 30 feet that divers should take after no-decompression dives to help reduce "silent bubbles" and the risk of pressure related injuries.

Scuba. The acronym for "self-contained underwater breathing apparatus." The word used to describe the equipment which consists of a demand regulator and a compressed air cylinder that is carried on the diver's back.

Second-Stage. The part of the regulator that fits in the diver's mouth, reduces the air pressure from 100-150 psi over ambient pressure, and supplies the air to the diver at breathing pressure on demand. Also known as regulator mouthpiece.

Snorkel. An open tube which extends from the mouth to the surface, and allows the snorkeler or scuba diver to breathe comfortably on the surface with the face in the water.

Snorkeling. Diving with the aid of mask, fins, snorkel, and BC and without the aid of scuba diving equipment. Also known as breath-hold diving, free diving, skin diving.

Squeeze. A condition of discomfort caused by a difference in pressure on an enclosed air space within the body or equipment: Ear, sinus, mask, suit.

Submersible Pressure Gauge (SPG). An instrument that is attached to the high-pressure port on the first-stage of the regulator and allows the diver to monitor how much air pressure remains in the scuba cylinder. Also known as pressure gauge.

Surface Interval (SI). The amount of time the diver stays out of the water or on the surface between dives, beginning as soon as the diver surfaces and ending at the start of the next descent.

Total Time (TT). The time divers must use to calculate their new repetitive group designation at the end of a repetitive dive. Calculated as Actual Time (AT) + Residual Time (RT) = Total Time (TT).

Turbid. Having sediment or foreign particles stirred up or suspended; muddy, cloudy, limited visibility.

Weight Belt. A device worn around the diver's waist and attached with a quick-release buckle, which allows the diver to offset the positive buoyancy caused by exposure suits.

Wet Suit. An exposure suit, commonly made of foam neoprene, which provides thermal insulation.

Index

Student Answer Sheet Directions

- Transfer your study guide answers to the following six Answer Sheet pages.

- Remember to write your name and the date on each page.

- Sign each page after you have reviewed each incorrect answer with your instructor.

- Your instructor will collect these pages during your Open Water Diver course.

STUDENT ANSWER SHEET

SCUBA SCHOOLS
INTERNATIONAL

STUDENT NAME   PART #   DATE

Reviewed and Corrected by Student and Instructor:

STUDENT SIGNATURE   INSTRUCTOR SIGNATURE

1. _____
2. _____
3. _____
4. _____
5. _____
6. _____
7. _____
8. _____
9. _____
10. _____
11. _____
12. _____
13. _____
14. _____
15. _____
16. _____
17. _____
18. _____
19. _____
20. _____

SSI STUDENT ANSWER SHEET

SCUBA SCHOOLS
INTERNATIONAL

STUDENT NAME _____   PART # _____ DATE _____

Reviewed and Corrected by Student and Instructor:

STUDENT SIGNATURE _____   INSTRUCTOR SIGNATURE _____

1. _____
2. _____
3. _____
4. _____
5. _____
6. _____
7. _____
8. _____
9. _____
10. _____
11. _____
12. _____
13. _____
14. _____
15. _____
16. _____
17. _____
18. _____
19. _____
20. _____

SSI STUDENT ANSWER SHEET

SCUBA SCHOOLS
INTERNATIONAL

STUDENT NAME _____ PART # _____ DATE _____

Reviewed and Corrected by Student and Instructor:

STUDENT SIGNATURE _____ INSTRUCTOR SIGNATURE _____

1. _____
2. _____
3. _____
4. _____
5. _____
6. _____
7. _____
8. _____
9. _____
10. _____
11. _____
12. _____
13. _____
14. _____
15. _____
16. _____
17. _____
18. _____
19. _____
20. _____

SSI STUDENT ANSWER SHEET

SCUBA SCHOOLS
INTERNATIONAL

STUDENT NAME   PART #   DATE

Reviewed and Corrected by Student and Instructor:

STUDENT SIGNATURE   INSTRUCTOR SIGNATURE

1. _____
2. _____
3. _____
4. _____
5. _____
6. _____
7. _____
8. _____
9. _____
10. _____
11. _____
12. _____
13. _____
14. _____
15. _____
16. _____
17. _____
18. _____
19. _____
20. _____

STUDENT ANSWER SHEET

SCUBA SCHOOLS
INTERNATIONAL

STUDENT NAME   PART #   DATE

Reviewed and Corrected by Student and Instructor:

STUDENT SIGNATURE   INSTRUCTOR SIGNATURE

---

1. _____
2. _____
3. _____
4. _____
5. _____
6. _____
7. _____
8. _____
9. _____
10. _____
11. _____
12. _____
13. _____
14. _____
15. _____
16. _____
17. _____
18. _____
19. _____
20. _____

SSI STUDENT ANSWER SHEET

SCUBA SCHOOLS
INTERNATIONAL

STUDENT NAME   PART #   DATE

Reviewed and Corrected by Student and Instructor:

STUDENT SIGNATURE   INSTRUCTOR SIGNATURE

1. _____
2. _____
3. _____
4. _____
5. _____
6. _____
7. _____
8. _____
9. _____
10. _____
11. _____
12. _____
13. _____
14. _____
15. _____
16. _____
17. _____
18. _____
19. _____
20. _____